Evangelizing the Hard-to-Reach

EVANGELIZING THE HARD-TO-REACH

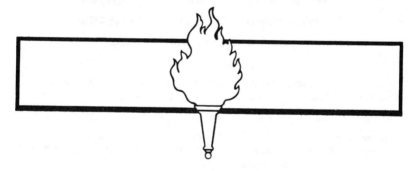

Robert D. Dale
Delos Miles

BROADMAN PRESS
Nashville, Tennessee

Unless otherwise noted, Scripture quotations are from the Revised Standard Version of the Bible, copyrighted 1946, 1952, © 1971, 1973.

Scripture quotations marked (KJV) are from the King James Version of the Bible.

Scripture quotations marked (NASB) are from the *New American Standard Bible.* Copyright © The Lockman Foundation, 1960, 1962, 1963, 1968, 1971, 1972, 1973, 1975, 1977. Used by permission.

Library of Congress Cataloging-in-Publication Data

Dale, Robert D.
    Evangelizing the hard-to-reach.

    (Broadman leadership series)
    1. Evangelistic work.   I. Miles, Delos.
II. Title.   III. Series.
BV3790.D24   1986   266   85-24262
ISBN 0-8054-6251-1 (pbk.)

To President W. Randall Lolley and Dean J. Morris Ashcraft of Southeastern Baptist Theological Seminary. In gratitude, because their outstanding administrative leadership makes our teaching ministries easier, and their Christian lives model the targeted evangelism approach described here.

Foreword

"Living off the easy ones." The phrase stuck in my mind. I was talking to a missions leader from a large southern city about the growth of the churches in his area. Whether transfer members or converts, the church growth picture was essentially the same. "The churches in my area, especially the suburban ones, are living off the easy ones," reported the missions leader.

Living off the easy ones. Theologically, the idea that any church would be content to settle for evangelizing only promptly responsive persons is heresy. Did Christ only die for those select persons who are saved after one or two hearings of the gospel? Not if you believe John 3:16.

Our interest in evangelizing hard-to-reach persons is personal as well as theological. Both of us were converted out of circumstances that had left us unattractive to the church or resistant to the gospel. Our testimonies are included later in this book. We're eternally grateful that some churches patiently and persistently reached out to us.

When congregations sensitize themselves to the hard-to-reach in their communities and tailor their outreach efforts to include those hard-to-reach persons, these churches will stop living off the easy ones.

Readers of this volume will recognize that we have used the term *evangelizing* with a broad application. We use the term to refer to proclaiming the good news to hard-to-reach non-Christians who have not professed faith in Jesus Christ as Lord and Savior. We also use the term to refer to sharing the gospel and its implications with those hard-to-reach Christians who have dropped out of service and fellowship and need to be encouraged to renew their commitments to Christ and His church. How we have used the term will be clear within the framework of each chapter.

Contents

1
Who Are the
Hard-to-Reach?: A Model

Is it possible? A Texas evangelism professor speculated on how contemporary churches might respond to the rich young ruler. "If most churches had the rich young ruler on their prospect list," the professor surmised, "they would baptize him in spite of his marginal interest and make him chairman of the Finance Committee!" Is it possible that many congregations are so focused on the easy-to-reach unchurched that they overlook or even ignore hard-to-reach persons?

Evangelizing hard-to-reach persons is a crucial ministry of any church. Hard-to-reach persons obviously aren't overly responsive to Christian witness. Some of these resistant persons counter the Holy Spirit's ripening process in their lives. Others are bypassed by churches because of selective outreach attempts. Whatever the reasons that evangelistic efforts aren't easily successful with the hard-to-reach, congregations can't concentrate on living off the easy-to-reach to the virtual exclusion of hard-to-reach persons. Why? Because Christ died for all. And because hard-to-reach persons make up a considerable portion of America's unchurched potential for evangelism.

Four Americans in ten are unchurched. That's about eighty million of our neighbors, sixty-one million of whom are eighteen or older.[1] Many of these unchurched folk fall into various hard-to-reach categories.

The unchurched are everywhere, though not equally distributed.[2] Ten of the fifteen states ranking highest in percentage of unchurched population are in the Rocky Mountain and Pacific

regions. The American West is our most heavily unchurched terri-
tory at 53.8 percent; the South is our most churched area with 34.3
percent claiming no church tie.

Eight states, primarily in the West, register a majority of their
population as unchurched: Oregon and Washington (60.9 percent
each), California (57 percent), Hawaii (56.2 percent), Alaska (56.1
percent), Nevada (53.6 percent), West Virginia (52 percent), and
Colorado (51.4 percent). East of the Mississippi River, West Virginia (#7), Maine (#9), Indiana (#12), Florida (#14), and New
Hampshire (#15) are in the fifteen least-churched state category.

On the other hand, only four states claim less than 20 percent
of their population unchurched: Utah (10.7 percent), Louisiana
(16.8 percent), and North Dakota and Rhode Island (17.8 percent
each).[3]

From an individual viewpoint, who's the most likely candidate
to be unchurched? Here's the profile:

- Male
- Young adult
- Unmarried
- Manual worker
- Not a high school graduate
- Living in a city of over 50,000 persons
- Residing in the Pacific Coast region[4]

But that's speaking statistically, of course. In truth, the churchless
American appears in an infinite variety of personalities and pla-
ces.[5]

Who Are the Churchless?

The *churchless American,* a term used interchangeably with *unchurched* throughout this book, refers to all persons outside the
church. Technically, churchless Americans are "persons who don't
participate in or feel a loyalty to the ongoing life of a local
church."[6] How do you think about participation in and loyalty to
a congregation? Here's what we observe. Lack of participation is

shown by no church attendance or activity. Lack of loyalty is indicated by no emotional involvement or commitment to a church. This definition is more behavioral than theological. Rather than depending on a person's statement of faith, we're observing how persons act toward Christ and the church and how congregations behave toward persons outside of those religious communities.

Churchless Americans have excluded themselves from church life or have been excluded by congregations. Exclusion has an ugly flavor, doesn't it? Literally, *exclude* is derived from a combination of "shut" and "out." On the active side of the spectrum, exclusion means to refuse admission, to expel, or to force out. Taken in a more passive sense, exclusion signifies to omit, to discard, or to leave uninvited. Sociologically, we can explain how some persons are excluded from churches. From a human perspective, we prefer others like ourselves in outlook and attitude. Theologically, we cannot justify excluding anyone from the Christian community. God loves all of His creatures and longs for their redemption.

A Model of Churchlessness

Churchlessness, or exclusion from a local church, is a two-way street for hard-to-reach persons. For instance, I can be unchurched by ignoring the church or by deciding to have nothing to do with Christian congregations. Or, a local church can leave me unchurched by benign neglect or by a policy stance of exclusion. Simply put, some people don't feel they can be included in a church or have chosen to stay out of church. Conversely, some churches don't reach out to some persons or have deliberately decided to keep some out.

How can we picture different hard-to-reach groups for study purposes and for shaping our evangelism strategies? Using a four-quadrant model, categories of unchurched persons can be described and outreach approaches tailored to their particular needs.

	Person passively excludes congregation	Person actively excludes congregation
Congregation passively excludes person(s)	LEFT-OUTS	DROP-OUTS
Congregation actively excludes person(s)	LOCKED-OUTS	OPT-OUTS

This model assumes dual responsibility for churchless Americans: unchurched persons themselves and exclusive churches. Since a Christian church is a voluntary association, either persons or congregations can hold attitudes or take actions which are, therefore, exclusionary.

Whether the exclusionary evaluations originate in the hard-to-reach or in a church or whether the exclusionary stances are passive or active, the result is the same. The tragic outcome? Someone is excluded from the Christian community. If I in my freedom turn away from a congregation, I must bear the responsibility for my attitudes and actions. The body of Christ, however, is commanded to reach out to and include "whosoever will." Healthy congregations try to include every person—hard-to-reach or easy-to-reach—within their spheres of witness, influence, and ministry.

Unwanted Ads

The four basic categories of churchless Americans can be described briefly. Perhaps these characterizations will give us "eyes to see" and "ears to hear" our unchurched neighbors.

The Left-Outs are largely invisible persons. These hard-to-reach folk ignore or take no initiative toward the church. Reciprocally, they have been judged as unattractive prospects and neglected by congregations. The Left-Outs are overlooked and unsought. They are the victims of an emotional barrier they or the churches have built. Handicapped persons, the poor, language groups, and migrant workers are some examples of Left-Outs.

The Drop-Outs are persons who hold membership in churches technically but have moved into inactivity on the fringes of the congregation. Anxiety-producing events have triggered their departure. Drop-Outs have taken some action to leave, and their congregations have allowed them to exit. Consequently, they are half in and half out of the church and are lost to productive and meaningful participation. Drop-Outs are technically affiliated but have become marginal in commitment. Consequently, Drop-Outs also fit into the larger hard-to-reach group.

The Locked-Outs are persons whose life-styles differ from the church's values or traditions. Seen as deviant in some way, they are excluded. Many Locked-Outs sense their overt exclusion and have little interest in a church. Addicts, sexual deviants, nontraditionalists, ex-convicts, and ethnic minorities are generally in the hard-to-reach category we refer to as Locked-Outs.

The Opt-Outs are persons who have decided on an active stance against faith or against religious standards. Therefore, they are experienced by churches as threatening. Their decision regarding the church makes them hard-to-reach because they are launched on an antireligion life course. Atheists, secularists, hedonists, and "recreationaholics" are illustrative of Opt-Outs.

Chapters 2 through 9 are four sets of pairs. Each of the four categories of hard-to-reach persons is explored and is paired with a chapter of case studies giving actual accounts of how each hard-to-reach type was successfully evangelized.

Grace and the Healthy Church

What will healthy churches do to bring hard-to-reach Americans to faith and fellowship? Theologically speaking, saving grace is the gift of God alone. But from a human perspective, healthy congregations must offer loving and aggressive witness to all persons who may respond to the gospel. In part, witnessing to the hard-to-reach demands that churches will identify them and tailor their evangelism efforts for these persons.

Several questions for healthy congregational evangelism are raised as long as four of ten Americans remain unchurched:

• Will our congregations need to repent of exclusionary attitudes and actions?
• Will our congregations need consciousness raising and sensitizing? Will we develop eyes to see and ears to hear our churchless neighbors?

- Will our congregations tailor a range of specific evangelism and ministry strategies for particular hard-to-reach audiences?
- Will our congregations need to offer training in targeted evangelism and ministry approaches?
- Will our local congregations cultivate a sense of holy unrest as long as there are churchless Americans?

Motivating for Outreach

Someone may ask, "Don't you run the risk of discouraging churches in their evangelism efforts when you name specific groups as 'hard-to-reach' persons?" Maybe. But our intent is just the opposite. By spotlighting hard-to-reach persons, we hope to encourage churches to identify their unchurched neighbors, to cultivate them, and to offer effective witness to them. We believe the Left-Outs, Drop-Outs, Locked-Outs, and Opt-Outs can be reached. They must be evangelized even if they are hard to reach.

Notes

1. J. Russell Hale, *Who Are the Unchurched?* (Washington, D.C.: Glenmary Research Center, 1977), pp. 2-3.
2. Ibid., p. 4.
   By regions, the ranking of unchurched stand:
   1. Pacific, 57.8%
   2. Mountain, 41.1%
   3. East North Central, 38%
   4. South Atlantic, 37.9%
   5. Middle Atlantic, 36.9%
   6. New England, 32.3%
   7. East South Central, 32.2%
   8. West South Central, 29.8%
   9. West North Central, 29.5%
3. Ibid., pp. 97-99.

4. David A. Roozen, *The Churched and the Unchurched in America: a Comparitive Profile* (Washington, D.C.: Glenmary Research Center, 1978), pp. 2-3.

5. Major resources on the churchless American include J. Russell Hale, *Who Are the Unchurched?* (Washington, D.C.: Glenmary Research Center, 1977); David A. Roozen, *The Church and the Unchurched in America* (Washington, D.C.: Glenmary Research Center, 1978); *The Unchurched American* by the Princeton Religion Research Center and Gallup Organization; Edward A. Rauff, *Why People Join the Church* (New York: Pilgrim Press, 1979); and George Gallup, Jr. and David Poling, *The Search for America's Faith* (Nashville: Abingdon Press, 1980). Additional material supplementing the major unchurched studies include Jackson W. Carroll, Douglas W. Johnson, and Martin E. Marty, *Religion in America: 1950 to the Present* (San Francisco: Harper and Row, 1979); Peter W. Williams, *Popular Religion in America,* (Englewood Cliffs, N.J.: Prentice-Hall, 1980); Dean R. Hoge and David A. Roozen, *Understanding Church Growth and Decline: 1950-1978* (New York: Pilgrim Press, 1979); and Carl S. Dudley, *Where Have All Our People Gone? New Choices for Old Churches* (New York: Pilgrim Press, 1979).

6. This definition of the unchurched person is similar to Hale, p. 10; Roozen, pp. 4-5; and Rauff, p. 11.

7. This model is an exclusion matrix. It's unusual in that all categories are negative.

This model grew out of a series of lectures on the unchurched in America which Bob Dale presented at Home Missions Week at Ridgecrest, North Carolina, during August 1981. Later, a chapter intended to apply this model to lay leaders in outreach was published. For that overview, see Robert D. Dale, "Through the Road to Enriched Fellowship," in *Equipping Deacons in Church Growth Skills,* Henry Webb, comp., and Terry A. Peck, ed. (Nashville: Convention Press, 1982), pp. 70-77.

2
The Left-Outs: Seeing the Unattractive

The Left-Outs rarely show up on a church's prospect list. These hard-to-reach persons are the nearly invisible, faceless persons who fade into the woodwork and hold no special attraction for a church. Like the man by the pool of Bethesda in John 5, the Left-Outs are often so much a part of the local scene that they almost disappear from view.

Left-Outs sense, *Church people aren't like me.* So they keep their distance. The churches size up the Left-Outs and feel they are different. These perceptions—by the Left-Outs and by congregations—create barriers to including Left-Outs in many churches.

Left-Outs are excluded by neglect, perception, invisibility, lack of attractiveness, or by mutually ignoring each other. Esteem, worth, and value—all perceived to be low—keep Left-Outs from approaching the church and keeps the congregation from seeking them.

The list of potential Left-Outs is long. The hard-to-reach Left-Outs include:
• Persons who are single
• Persons who are deaf and others with communicative disorders
• Persons who are blind or visually impaired
• Persons who are mentally retarded
• Persons who are wheelchair users or with limited mobility
• Persons who are learning disabled
• Poor and economically down-and-outs
• Language groups
• Mobile-home dwellers

- Apartment dwellers
- Migrant workers
- Persons who are socially and culturally alienated
- Persons who are aged
- Persons who are painfully shy or introverted
- Persons who can't read
- Persons who are disfigured
- Persons who work night shifts

Grouping the Left-Outs

Three subgroups sum up the Left-Out category. The hand-icapped, the economically marginal, and the culturally alienated are clusters of the Left-Outs.

The Handicapped

The full array of physical and emotional handicaps create barriers to the Left-Outs feeling included in churches. Very few churches attempt to evangelize handicapped persons. For example, among North Carolina's 3,500 Southern Baptist churches, we know of 70 deaf ministries, 50 mentally retarded ministries, and only 1 blind ministry.[1]

The deaf. Two million Americans are completely deaf, and a much larger number is hearing impaired. Many churches sign their worship services to deaf worshipers; other churches provide amplifiers in the pews. Deafness is not as great a stigma as most other physical handicaps, and, therefore, churches are somewhat responsive in ministering to deaf persons. For example, the only college-level education for deaf students in North Carolina is in a Baptist college, Gardner-Webb.

The blind. Worldwide there are 15 million blind persons. We have 6.4 million visually impaired and about a half million blind Americans among our citizenry. On a national level, the John Milton Society helps churches establish ministries to blind persons, and the American Bible Society provides free braille Bibles to blind persons who can't afford a copy of the Scriptures.

Cecil Etheredge, consultant on ministries to visually handicapped, estimates about 37,000 Southern Baptists are visually impaired, or roughly one per church.[2] In our state of North Carolina, only one church and one association provide a specific ministry to blind persons. Are congregations in your state reaching out to visually handicapped persons? There is no real barrier to blind folk responding to Christ; only a congregation's perception of their visual handicap keeps the blind from being considered attractive prospects for outreach.

The wheelchair users. Nearly 5 million American adults are disabled. When a wheelchair-user friend recently moved to Raleigh, North Carolina, he found only one Baptist church with full accessibility to all its buildings and grounds for wheelchairs. New church structures are required by building codes to provide ramps, elevators, and rest room facilities for physically handicapped persons. It's a shame architectural codes have been more sensitive to our less physically mobile neighbors than has Christian love.

The mentally retarded. There are 7 million mentally retarded citizens in the United States. Less than 1 percent of our mentally retarded neighbors attend any church. Since 90 percent of the mentally retarded reside in their own homes and require close care, few of their family members attend church either. As many as 20 million Americans may be Left-Outs because congregations generally neglect mentally retarded persons.

A Greensboro, North Carolina, church has discovered a new area of outreach through a mentally retarded youngster. Consider this unusual story of Marie and the Joy Class:

> About ten years ago as our nominating committee was working on a new slate of officers and teachers for a new church year they were faced with the possible loss of one of two faithful workers. These two were a husband and wife

active in two departments and parents of a mentally retarded daughter, Marie.

Marie had been coming to church all of her life but had now, as often happens, realized she was different from her classmates who were younger and smaller than she, yet were able to do things that she was unable to do. So she rebelled—she just wasn't going to church anymore.

After sharing this experience with the nominating committee, the committee began to see a need for reaching out to meet Marie's needs and in so doing formed what came to be called the Joy Class. From one member on the first Sunday, the class has now grown to fourteen members made up for the most part of students who are severely to moderately retarded. Although they are limited in their capabilities, they are not limited in their enthusiasm as evidenced by their attendance and offering every Sunday morning.

We have seen Marie emerge from the unhappy child who didn't want to go to the church anymore to a young lady who goes up to neighbors, delivery men, or whoever, inviting them to church, where she is in attendance every service. She takes "her church" seriously, listening to her mother as she read the Bible through this past year. She is so pleased that she was asked to hand out the reports at business conference every month.

The Joy Class has participated in worship service to emphasize mental retardation month, and they love to sing for opening assembly in other Sunday School departments.

The first of December each year our church sponsors a party for the student body of McIver School, a special school for handicapped children in the Greensboro city school district. The Joy Class members act out the nativity scene, with one member reading the Scriptures. This is one of the highlights of the year for our entire church.

Tragically, however, the mentally retarded and their families are too often overlooked.

The Economically Marginal

I'll never forget the stir caused in our church by the visit of a multimillionaire's son. He became outreach prospect number one. His money made him a real celebrity in our midst, although he was embarrassed by our middle-class commotion over him. Sadly, I must admit we never got that excited over a poverty-stricken prospect. Poor persons are often Left-Outs where the church is concerned; we see them as burdens rather than resources.

The poor. Persons at or below the poverty level and elderly Americans on fixed incomes often see themselves as less than welcome by churches. Recently a retired man pleaded with me to help older church members realize that they can contribute other resources to their congregations besides money. After further conversation, I discovered this longtime churchman felt so limited by health and a tithe of many fewer dollars that he was struggling to feel wanted in his own church.

Several years ago, a widow living on a small pension while she reared two sons told me: "I have no money to give." I convinced her that her Bible teaching ability and her sons' religious education were more important to our church than money. She began coming to our church for worship. Within a year, I baptized both of her sons. Later, she and I agreed her sons' religious commitments were more crucial than any amount of money she could have given. Earlier, however, her meager income and her perception of the church as a status-conscious institution caused this widow to feel left out. And for several years previously, our congregation had been willing to omit this poor family from our outreach effort. We delivered our Christmas basket to them each year and otherwise ignored them. Both of the widow's sons were saved and baptized during the first year our congregation deliberately reached out to this family.

The migrant. Interstate migrants are part of a largely invisible underculture in America. Last winter an urban wanderer froze to death in an abandoned building in downtown Raleigh. The media did an investigation of the urban migrant problem and discovered a sizable group of floaters in the Triangle area. One enterprising vagrant was even renting cardboard "rooms" under a railroad trestle. An Episcopal church in downtown Raleigh responded to these migrants and opened a soup kitchen ministry. The congregation fed one hundred persons each lunch hour during the winter months.

Hard-core street people live a Gypsylike life-style that makes them hard-to-reach. Most street people are white males in their mid-thirties. Most are loners and alcoholics. Some suffer from emotional problems; many are simply "down on their luck."

Additionally, a mobile tribe of interstate farm workers estimated at 25 thousand travels through our state of North Carolina each year. What are the statistics for your state? These food harvesters live in 700 camps scattered throughout the state and earn in the neighborhood of $3,000 yearly. While serving an interim pastorate in eastern North Carolina, I discovered about 6 thousand migrant farm workers picked vegetables in that one county annually. When I inquired about the migrants, the farmers themselves were only vaguely aware of this rootless host and were surprised by the sheer number of these mostly Black and Hispanic persons.

Basic health needs provide an entry point to ministry with migrants. The average life expectancy of a migrant farm worker is only forty-nine years. The birth mortality rate is three times as high as the general population. Migrants are twice as apt to die of flu or pneumonia as the national average.[3] Yet, when a pastor friend worked to provide pure drinking water for broomcorn cutters camped near his church in Oklahoma, he was roundly criticized by area churches for suspicious and radical activity. A cup of unpolluted water in Christ's name seems like an avenue to Christian evangelism to us.

Congregations recognize how difficult reaching mobile populations is. But "the stranger within thy gates" was a consistent object of care in our Old Testament heritage (see Ex. 20:10). First Baptist Church, Cowpens, South Carolina, is ministering successfully to migrant farm workers. And the Southside Baptist Church in Fulton, Missouri, is providing church members trained as counselors to minister to Missouri's largest truck stop, a service area for 10 thousand truckers each week.

The Culturally Alienated

An increasing number of Americans feel out-of-sync with our nation's social atmosphere. On the one hand, political groups lobby nostalgically for what they perceive as simpler times and more traditional values. On the other hand, language groups and young adults still experiencing the out-of-jointedness of the seventies feel left out of our culture too.

The language groups. Immigrants to America's melting pot used to be predominantly European. But with an annual influx of 400 thousand legal immigrants, today's new Americans are increasingly in the Hispanic and Asian language groups. For example, 1 thousand Mexicans are entering Houston each month, changing its Old South culture to a south-of-the-border outlook. Los Angeles now has 1.5 million citizens of Latin-American origins, as well as the United States largest Korean community.[4] Former Cuban refugees own 8 thousand businesses in Dade County, Florida, and pump 1.5 billion dollars a year into the Miami area economy. Miami is now 78 percent ethnic. Where churches persist in extending the gospel only in English, many Americans are excluded from our outreach efforts. They are Left-Outs and are hard-to-reach.

The mobile church member. Americans are migratory folk, moving on the average of thirteen times during their life-times. One family out of five moves each year. When church members from the South move into parts of the United States where their denomination's work is still taking root, many have difficulty fitting into a new congregation. Instead of fine church buildings and elaborate programs, these mobile Christians often find storefront churches. Disillusioned and culture shocked or glad to be out of the Bible Belt, they may join other denominations. One Southern Baptist college graduate, a lifelong Baptist church member and former denominational worker, joined a Presbyterian church. The report? About one hundred of the two hundred members in his Sunday School class were former Baptists.[5]

Mobile church members who begin to show signs of alienation are soon left alone by their own churches. An estimated 70 thousand Southern Baptists are living in the state of New York but haven't affiliated with a Southern Baptist church.

Single adults. The fastest growing segment of the American population is singles—never married, divorced, or widowed. One third of the nation's population, or nearly 75 million Americans eighteen years or older, are single. Dallas, Atlanta, Chicago, and New York have nearly half of their populations made up of singles.[6] Many churches are suspicious of singles. When single persons in their mid-twenties encounter church members, they may sense or even hear the question: Why aren't you married?

The social alien. A subgroup of hard-to-define Left-Outs is the social alien. Mostly single young adults, these persons have a vague uneasiness about churchmanship. Some of them bear the imprint of the 1970s social conscience. Many of them have deep religious feelings, but they wonder if they're out of step with their churches. Usually unmarried and somewhat secular in their lifestyle, the social aliens are often Left-Outs and are especially hard-to-reach.

Human Pain and God's Healing

Evangelism has both relational and theological dimensions. Salvation is fundamentally theological: It's God's primary work and His alone. But the saving grace of Christ is communicated relationally—through the witness of believers. Paul's statement of the relational-theological foundations for outreach is classic: "God was in Christ reconciling the world to himself, . . . So we are ambassadors for Christ, God making his appeal through us" (2 Cor. 5:19-20).

One way to think about reaching specific groups of persons with an effective witness, therefore, is to think of the group's basic relational and theological needs. What is their baseline need for human relationships? What theological theme speaks to their core needs most powerfully? When these questions are answered for a hard-to-reach group, strategies for evangelism can be tailored to that group.

Left-Outs need friendship. They feel no one really cares for them—not even church people. Physically or emotionally handicapped persons feel unattractive and worthless. They want to sense "we're alike" from other human beings in spite of physical or mental differences. Most of all, handicapped folk want to know their Creator continues to recreate His people and make us whole.

Economically marginal persons feel they have nothing to offer, are uninteresting, and are without status. They need others who will relate to them without reference to socioeconomic classifications. They want a "you're like me" relationship with people regardless of income level. If the ground really is level at the foot of the Cross, as we've preached so long, classlessness should be a natural aspect of congregational life. God values all of His creatures equally; Christ died for all—the rich and the beggar at the gate.

Culturally alienated persons feel too different and distanced from society and the church's mainstream. They need to see we who follow Christ aren't stained-glass saints. They want to know we are tempted and feel the pressures of society's ills too. Befriending the alienated may help us discover some secular saints who are trying to heal our culture's sicknesses and would be even more effective with the resources of the Great Physician. An "I'm like you" sense can open the communication channels for an effective witness.

The Left-Outs feel they don't fit in or can't belong. Such feelings of exclusion contradict *koinonia*. Christ has demolished the dividing walls (Eph. 2:14; Gal. 3:28). The early church effectively included the entire spectrum of humanity within its fellowship (Acts 2:9-11,41; 5:32-39; 6:5-7). Today's church can't exclude Left-Outs just because some subgroups are small or difficult to reach. We have no mandate to build barriers to the gospel that our Savior earlier tore down.

Including the Left-Outs

Awareness of Left-Out groups and their hurts suggests several outreach strategies. While these approaches are mainstream evangelistic techniques, they are especially suited to reaching Left-Outs.

Exclusive Mind-set Must Change

Churches traditionally spend 90 percent of their efforts trying to reach 50 percent of their prospects. To reach the Left-Outs, this exclusive mind-set must be confronted and changed. We might be surprised by how responsive some Left-Out groups will be to the gospel.

Left-Outs Are Susceptible to Love

Because the Left-Outs have been largely ignored and neglected, genuine interest and recognition has a terrific impact on them. When Jesus noted that the sick need a physician, He reminded us that persons who recognize their own needs are more responsive to care. No message is more central than Christ's love; no life-style is more demanding than loving others like Christ loved us.

Koinonia Must Be Developed

Churches can become cliquish. Cliques are the opposite of *koinonia,* the New Testament ideal for the atmosphere of a local congregation. Cliques are generally the perversion of a human's natural need to belong. That is, we all need to belong. But once we feel we're "in," we may close ranks and keep the outs "out."

In America, our pluralistic culture has operated on the principle that our differences enrich us. The biblical idea of *koinonia* underscores the same concept. In fact, *koinonia* demands differences to prove itself. Mere homogeneity isn't *koinonia,* its basis, or its result.

Specialized Ministries

Constructive ministries to handicapped persons or language groups require specialized skills and mature attitudes. Many of these special programs grow initially out of the interest of one person or a small group. Churches need to guard against enlisting leaders for specialized ministries whose need to be loved overwhelms their ability to love others in Christ's name.

Eyes to See

None of God's creatures deserve to be Left-Outs. And they won't be if congregations will sensitize themselves with eyes which really see and ears which really hear the universal need to be befriended in Christ's name.

The concern of Jesus for common people should become our model. If 15 million handicapped Americans can work productively, why aren't churches attracted to them too? Are middle-class congregations becoming so upwardly mobile that we're class conscious to the neglect of our poor neighbors? Are we modeling church life too exclusively on the super-churches when, in fact, most American congregations are rather small in membership and modest in resources? God forbid that Christians should confuse the American dream of success with the gospel of salvation and service. When "big, new, fast, and fancy" replace witness, love, service, and humility, your congregation and mine are apt to overlook the Left-Outs.

Notes

1. At a denominational level, Southern Baptists make a minimal effort to reach out to and teach handicapped persons. The Sunday School Board's 1984-85 Church Materials catalog lists one page (out of a total of 136 pages) of "special ministry materials." Two items for the blind, three resources for the mentally retarded, six supplies for the deaf, and two additional general resource pieces are advertised. These materials emphasize teaching more than reaching handicapped persons. Some other materials are available through state convention missions departments and other agencies.

2. "High Visibility for the Blind," *Home Missions Notebook*, (Spring 1981), p. 6.

3. These statistics are drawn from "Migrant Farm Workers," a Light and Leaven series pamphlet available from the Council on Christian Life and Public Affairs, Box 26508, Raleigh, NC.

4. This information is from "Language Missions Data," Department of Language Missions, Home Mission Board, SBC, n.d.

5. Norman Jameson, "Move May Result in Culture Shock," *Baptist Digest*, 27 Apr. 1981, pp. 1, 3.

6. "Singles Offer Church Ministry Opportunity," *Baptist Digest*, 8 Aug. 1983, p. 8.

3
Case Studies of Evangelized Left-Outs

Biblical cases of Left-Outs may include the man who had been ill for thirty-eight years (John 5:2-18); the man born blind (John 9:1-41); the paralytic carried by four men (Mark 2:1-12); and Bartimaeus the blind beggar outside of Jericho (Mark 10:46-52).[1] We offer three contemporary cases in this chapter: two of whom were known to be economically marginal and among the poor; one of whom was handicapped by blindness, brain tumor, and confined to a wheelchair. Most likely, all three were of low esteem, worth, and value in their own eyes and in the eyes of congregations. Each of the three was to some extent socially alienated. The case of Anty may have also been used in the Locked-Out or Drop-Out categories, though we think it fits best here.

"Look Who His Father Was": The Case of Delos Miles[2]

I happened to overhear an outstanding church member say to another man when I was about nine or ten, "Delos will never amount to anything. Look who his father was!"

My parents were not Christians, nor were they practicing members of any religious group. I grew up in an atmosphere of both spiritual and physical poverty. My father could neither read nor write. In fact, he had to sign his name with an X. My mother had a third grade education.

Daddy was a day laborer who worked one day for what we ate the next. Only the last year of his life was he promoted from a common farm laborer to a tobacco sharecropper.

By that time, there were four of us children to feed, clothe, and care for.

We were on the bottom rung of the social and economic ladder, if indeed on the ladder at all. I recall how my older sister and I would at times steal chickens from the people on whose farms we lived. The first pair of shoes I remember owning was a secondhand pair of brogans given to me by my first-grade schoolteacher. I was very proud of those shoes.

Often we were hungry and cold, and always without adequate clothes and housing. Daddy was also addicted to alcohol.

My mother left us when I was seven. She took my baby sister and never returned, except to attend father's funeral. Shortly after my eighth birthday, my father was murdered in a drunken brawl. He was stabbed and cut to death by one of his best friends.

When I lost my father, my whole world caved in. I thought my mother had hired my dad's friend to kill him. My heart was filled with hatred, and my mind was wounded from so many hurts. I had no place to go. My relatives didn't want me.

Then, after a few months, something very good happened to me. I was invited to live with people I knew. For the first time in my life, I had a bed of my own, three good meals every day, and decent clothes and shoes.

More important, however, than all these material blessings was the fact that these folk were believers in Jesus Christ and members of the Baptist church in that rural community. They took me to church with them.

In that open country church, I discovered the Bible, a book to which I was almost a total stranger, although I had been born and reared in what is called the Bible Belt. Now I learned about God in worship services, Sunday School, prayer meetings, Vacation Bible School, Royal Ambassadors, and youth groups.

When I was eleven years old, I felt separated from God. There was a miserable feeling inside of me. I was so unhappy I felt I was going to die. I talked this over with my Sunday School teacher and with my foster parents. They all told me to ask God to forgive my sin.

As best I knew, I invited Christ to be my Savior and Lord. That unhappy feeling left me. Peace and joy came into my life. I publicly professed my faith in Jesus Christ and later was baptized.

I grew in grace and in favor with God and persons until my fourteenth birthday. At that time, I was reconciled to my mother. I became convinced that she had nothing to do with my father's death and that she did in fact love me very much.

I left my foster home and went to live with my mother and stepfather in Charleston, South Carolina. Shortly after arriving there, I discovered that my stepfather drank a great deal. Life was unpleasant in that environment. So at the age of fourteen, I quit school and joined the United States Army.

When the Korean conflict broke out in 1950, I was on an assignment in Japan. Instead of coming back home, I was sent to Korea.

My platoon was overrun by Chinese soldiers on the night of November 27, 1950. I lay in a bunker for over eighteen hours without consciously moving a muscle in my body. Wounded in the hand and the head, I lay there slowly bleeding and freezing almost to death. Two Chinese soldiers were in the bunker with me all night long. I silently confessed my sins to God, promising if He would get me out of that situation I would serve Him the rest of my life.

God did bring me out after three days and nights. Only seven men from my entire company survived. I spent nine months in various hospitals undergoing treatment and sur-

gery. At first I thought I would never walk again because my
feet had frozen and turned black up to the ankles.

God healed all of these deep hurts in my life. He healed
me of feelings of rejection toward my mother; of grief over
the separation of my parents; of hatred toward my father's
murderer; of grief over his death; of an inferiority complex
about my social, economic, and educational status in society;
of bitterness and ill will toward North Koreans and Chinese;
of gunshot wounds and severely frostbitten feet; and, above
all, of the cancer of sin.

I have chosen as the golden text of my life Proverbs 3:5-6:
"Trust in the Lord with all your heart,/and do not rely on
your own insight./In all your ways acknowledge him,/and
he will make straight your paths."

I no longer desire much to "amount to anything." Because
of what God has done for me through Jesus Christ, I know
I am a royal member of the family of God. Like Paul, I want
persons to regard me as a servant of Jesus Christ and a stew-
ard of the mysteries of God (1 Cor. 4:1). But it would please
me if they could say, "Look who his Father is!"

Commentary on "Look Who His Father Was"

No church actively excluded me and my parental family. Nor
did we actively exclude any church. The two or three times I
remember going to church prior to age eight were with the Pen-
tecostal Holiness people. Of course, I didn't know or care anything
about denominations then.

Probably we felt more comfortable with the Pentecostals because they were our kind of people. Yet no church of any kind
actively sought to include us. Passivity on their part and ours was
characteristic.

According to John 4, Jesus assumed the role of host with the
woman at the well. He treated the woman of Samaria as a guest
in her country. Jesus took the initiative in that conversation. He

asked of her a drink of well water but offered her living water. If we Christians pattern our evangelizing after Jesus, we shall take the initiative in putting strangers at ease in our midst.[3]

There was a sense in which my family and I were strangers within the congregations' courts and beggars at their gates. Day laborers on the farms were more like migrants than any other group. Even the higher-class sharecroppers frequently moved every year or two. What we needed was someone to break down the walls which separated us from the churches, a friend who drew a circle of love big enough to include us along with everybody else.

My foster parents drew that larger circle of love for me. They voluntarily took in a welfare kid who didn't have any other place to go. Freely they shared with me their material, cultural, and spiritual wealth. We should not overlook the Christian foster home as one means for evangelizing today's Left-Outs.

Nor should we belittle the role of public worship and the church organizations in conveying the gospel. Although I was born and reared in what some call the buckle of the Bible Belt, I was as ignorant of the gospel as the cave dwellers were of computers.

Those five or six years between the ages of eight and fourteen spent in regular worship attendance, Sunday School, Vacation Bible School, Royal Ambassadors, and other church youth groups such as Baptist Young People's Training Union (BYPU) so indelibly wrote the gospel on my heart that I hope never to return to the BC of my life. The gospel which sustained me through the ordeal of the Korean War was the same good news I first heard in an open country church. That gospel with which I first began to get acquainted at age eight in a Sunday School class is still "the power of God for salvation to every one who has faith" (Rom. 1:16).

"Blind and Nearly Bald": The Case of Minnie[4]

My most unforgettable witnessing experience was an apparent failure that later turned into a beautiful example of *oikos* evangelism.[5]

I had been asked some weeks prior to come and witness to a twelve-year-old little girl who was dying from a brain tumor. I made the visit, and the child responded by asking Christ into her heart. Time and circumstances prohibited me from sharing with the remainder of the family who were all lost. I asked the mother if I could return another time and talk to the rest of the family. She said she would like that and for me to come anytime.

The next week I took two church members with me and returned to the home. Minnie, the little girl, was present, and we talked for about an hour. She said she had been telling everybody about Jesus and how much He loved them. The mother called the other three daughters into the room to listen to what we had to say. I was convinced that each of them would accept Christ that evening. The youngest boy kept running through the room trying to get attention. In spite of the distraction, I shared the gospel message as effectively as I knew how. After sharing the message, I looked at the mother and asked her if there was anything to keep her from committing her life to Christ that evening. She looked blankly into my face and said, "I'm just not ready." Each of the daughters made a similar response.

I was shocked at the response of the family. The mother had been so concerned for her daughter's salvation but was not ready herself to be saved. I had assumed too much. We made conversation for a while longer and asked if we could return another time. We received a positive response and left.

The mother began bringing the girls to church over the next few weeks and months. During this time, Minnie asked to be baptized. What a sight that was! Confined to a wheelchair, blind, and nearly bald, Minnie sat smiling and tapping her foot as the soloist sang "Turn Your Eyes upon Jesus." As two men lifted her out of her wheelchair to lower her to me in the baptismal pool, a lady asked her if she were afraid they might drop her. Minnie replied, "They might drop me, but Jesus will never drop me." Minnie died not many weeks after her baptism. I was asked to preach the funeral and did.

Two weeks after the funeral, two of the three daughters came forward during the invitation time on Sunday morning. Several weeks later the third daughter came forward. Each had accepted Christ and desired to be baptized and accepted for church membership. Several more weeks passed, and the mother accepted Christ and followed in baptism and church membership. Not long afterward, the husband of the oldest daughter accepted Christ, and he too sought baptism and church membership.

One of the daughters shared that she had been under conviction since that night we visited in their home. She had wanted to accept Christ that evening but felt inhibited by her mother and sisters being present.

It had seemed like a failure at first, but God accomplished what He wanted done in the family of a little blind, dying girl.

Commentary on "Blind and Nearly Bald"

There is no evidence in the case that the church had actively excluded Minnie or her family. Apparently she and her family had not actively excluded the church. Passivity on both sides seems to have been the order of the day here until an impending crisis.

The crisis? A twelve-year-old girl was dying of a brain tumor, and she was not a disciple. The case points to a theological crisis accentuated by a physical crisis.

We are not told who asked the preacher to go and witness to Minnie. Did Minnie's mother initiate the visit? That would help us to understand the pastor's shock at the initially negative response of Minnie's mother and sisters. If the mother initiated the request, that may have signaled the family's shift to an active stance toward the church.

If someone from the pastor's congregation issued the request for a witnessing visit, that was a healthy sign that at least one or more of the church members actively wanted to include Minnie and her family. That kind of request, however, would raise some question about the adequacy of lay witnessing.

From whomever came the request, an important point to note is that under the pastor's leadership the church changed from a passive stance toward Minnie and her family to an active host. He made a home visit and the next week returned with two church members. After that, the mother started bringing her girls to church. Doesn't that look more like Great Commission evangelism than the kind that passively excludes persons?[6]

Active, inclusive evangelism frequently results in the salvation of a network of persons. Minnie became a Christian. Two weeks after her funeral, two of her sisters confessed faith in Christ and joined the church. Later, the third daughter and the mother did likewise. Not long afterward, the husband of the oldest daughter followed in their steps. See how the gospel moved forward through that web of kinship and deep relationships.

"Locked into the Welfare Cycle": The Case of Anty[7]

Antoinette died of multiple brain tumors and cancer in 1979. Those who knew her well affectionately called her Anty. When home missionary Bruce Schoonmaker first met Anty at the Graffiti Center in Manhattan, New York, she seemed to be without hope. Locked into the welfare cycle with two small daughters to support, Anty drank beer constantly. She could hardly hold a coherent thread of thought and shouted a lot at her girls.

Schoonmaker's first contact with Anty came through a puppet show which he was conducting to enlist persons in

Bible studies. That puppet show touched something deep inside of her. She began attending a Bible study at the center and became an ardent supporter of the center's programs.

Anty belonged to a local Catholic church. She asked Schoonmaker, a Baptist missionary, to hold Bible studies in her home which was often a gathering place for a lot of persons who watched TV and drank beer. Some of Anty's Catholic friends tried to get her to quit fraternizing with Baptists, but she indignantly rejected their efforts.

Over the next two years, Anty attended Baptist Bible studies. She changed very slowly, but in 1978 she gave up beer, and her mind became clear. She began to be more regular in attending her own church. Schoonmaker questioned her about salvation. Her reply indicated she had become a Christian, although she knew nothing of conservative evangelical language.

Anty continued over the next months to grow spiritually, mentally, and improve physically. She became a catechism teacher and began to work with young Catholic girls. She remained loyal to both the Baptists and the Catholics until her untimely death.

Schoonmaker was asked to say a few words about Antoinette at her Catholic funeral. Part of what he said was: "She put her faith and trust in God. Anty was not perfect— none of us is—however, she was growing in wholeness in God."

Commentary on "Locked into the Welfare Cycle"

An art form as simple as a puppet show may be used of God to touch something deep inside of some Left-Outs. It worked with Anty. We need some point of contact with Left-Outs. Not all of them are interested in Sunday School or any other church program organization. Christian artists might be able to help us reach some

Left-Outs. Certain cities, such as New York and Washington, D.C., have Christian arts groups who may be able to assist us.[8]

Bible study also played a role in evangelizing Anty. Because of the puppet show, she began to attend Bible study at the Graffiti Center. Later, Anty invited the Baptist home missionary to hold Bible studies in her home.[9] Churches should not overlook weekday Bible studies conducted in homes and other nonchurch turf settings in their strategy for reaching Left-Outs.

The case implies that the Graffiti Center was involved in a holistic approach to Christian mission and ministry which bridged evangelism and social involvement. Anty grew spiritually, mentally, and improved physically. That reminds us of the Scripture which says, "Jesus increased in wisdom and in stature, and in favor with God and man" (Luke 2:52). Churches which view evangelism and Christian social involvement as two wings of the same bird may be better prepared to reach Left-Outs like Anty.

The human instrument God used to evangelize Anty was non-judgmental in his dealings with her. If Schoonmaker had been judgmental, do you think Anty would have opened her heart and home to him? If he had demanded that she stop drinking beer immediately, instantly cease shouting at her girls, get off of welfare, and cease going to her own church, how far do you think he would have gotten with this Left-Out? Are we nonjudgmental in our dealings with Left-Outs?

Suppose Schoonmaker had insisted on Anty's use of "conservative evangelical language"? Would he have gotten as far as first base in evangelizing her using "evangelicalese"? Have you ever thought it strange that we spend millions of dollars teaching our foreign missionaries the language of their host country but don't bother much to teach home missionaries the language of their target groups? If we pattern our evangelizing after Jesus Christ in His incarnation, we shall make every effort to communicate with Left-Outs in a language they can understand.

The case also depicts conversion and the Christian life as a process. Anty was not perfect even at the time of her death. Missionary Schoonmaker said, "She was growing in wholeness in God." Although a member of a local Catholic church, Anty "seemed to be without hope" when we first meet her. "She changed very slowly, but in 1978 she gave up beer, and her mind became clear." Churches and Christians who think of conversion and the Christian life as more like a spiral where the death angel passes over again and again may be more apt to evangelize the Antoinettes of their communities.[10]

Notes

1. The first three of these cases are analyzed in separate chapters of Delos Miles, *How Jesus Won Persons* (Nashville: Broadman Press, 1982), pp. 75-83,84-93, and 113-121.

2. This is a condensed and recast version of the spiritual biography published in Delos Miles, *Introduction to Evangelism* (Nashville: Broadman Press, 1983), pp. 167-175.

3. For more information on hospitality evangelism, we recommend Bruce A. Rowlison, *Creative Hospitality as a Means of Evangelism* (Campbell, Calif.: Green Leaf Press, 1981). The address is P. O. Box 5, Campbell, CA 95009.

4. This case was written by one of our students, Rev. Dave Darbyshire, in the fall of 1983 and is used with his permission.

5. *Oikos* is the Greek word for house or household. One's *oikos* in the first century included spouse, children, extended family members, and even slaves and other workers. The term is now used to refer to one's sphere of influence or one's web of relationships with kin, friends, and associates. We recommend the following books relating to *oikos* evangelism: Ron Johnson, Joseph W. Hinkle, Charles M. Lowry, *Oikos: A Practical Approach to Family Evangelism* (Nashville: Broadman Press, 1982); Win Arn and Charles Arn, *The Master's Plan for Making Disciples* (Pasadena, Calif.: Church Growth Press, 1982); W. Oscar Thompson, Jr., *Concentric Circles of*

Concern (Nashville: Broadman Press, 1981); and Delos Miles, *How Jesus Won Persons.*

6. For help in the diagnosis and treatment of passive congregations we recommend Lyle E. Schaller, *Activating the Passive Church* (Nashville: Abingdon, 1981).

7. This case is based on "Courage to Continue: His Answer Is Anty," *Home Missions Notebook,* 2, No. 4, (Winter, 1981), p. 15.

8. See Carol R. Thiessen, "Christian Artists on the Outs Form Their Own In Groups," *Christianity Today,* 27, No. 16, 1983 Oct. 21, p. 46.

9. For help in conducting evangelistic Bible studies, see Delos Miles, "Evangelistic Bible Studies," *Introduction to Evangelism,* pp. 345-354.

10. For more on the spiral model of conversion, we recommend Orlando E. Costas, "Conversion as a Complex Experience: A Personal Case Study," *Gospel & Culture,* eds. John Stott and Robert T. Coote (Pasadena: Wm. Carey Library, 1979), pp. 240-262.

4
The Drop-Outs: Forsaking the Assembly

Church Drop-Outs—folk whose names are on church rolls but whose hearts and bodies live outside their congregations—aren't a new issue for the Christian community. Some of Jesus' earliest followers abandoned Him. The Fourth Gospel notes, "After this many of his disciples drew back and no longer went about with him" (John 6:66). Judas deserted Jesus permanently. Simon Peter abandoned Jesus temporarily (Luke 22:54-62). Paul discovered the drop-out syndrome with John Mark (Acts 13:13) and Demas (2 Tim. 4:10). The writer of Hebrews also recognized the drop-out phenomenon and urged believers to keep on worshiping and fellowshiping together (Heb. 10:25). But Drop-Outs have continued to forsake the Christian assembly.

Drop-out church members still hold formal membership in congregations but have receded into inactivity on the fringes of their churches. They are suspended half in and half out of their churches and are lost to productive and meaningful participation. Drop-Outs are technically affiliated but marginally committed. They are hard-to-reach members.

In general, Drop-Outs are excluded from Christian service by their response to life disruptions, religious burnout, and church fights. Persons who are prime candidates to drop out of local churches include:
• Persons who don't like their new pastor
• New high school graduates
• Persons who didn't like the way the last pastor left
• Single youth

- Persons who have recently moved
- Empty-nest couples
- Persons who were wounded in congregational conflicts
- Religious burnouts
- Persons whose life patterns have been seriously disrupted
- Viewers of the electronic church

Decision + Permission = Gone

Drop-Outs are usually the result of persons' decisions to cut back on their participation level which was triggered by an anxiety- or anger-causing event. Their churches allow them to leave by not retrieving them immediately. Whether it's an "I-need-a-sabbatical" attitude or someone leaving in a huff, members' participation and loyalty are lost to their congregation. When church members drop out, there's a ripe time for reinvolving the Drop-Out. One study discovered an eight-to-ten week "window of waiting."[1] During this time frame, the Drop-Outs wait for someone to pay attention to them or to correct the situation which caused them to leave their church. Often a visit by the pastor or a concerned layperson can motivate a return to active participation. If, however, Drop-Outs are ignored, their energies and interests are soon reinvested to other volunteer activities or individual concerns. They then become long-term Drop-Outs.

After about a year of withdrawal and reinvestment has passed, Drop-Outs' feelings regarding their congregation cool, and they become highly resistant to change.[2] They have dropped out and a new life pattern without church involvement has stabilized. The implication is clear: To regain inactive members, congregations must seek out their Drop-Outs quickly and directly. If action to retrieve Drop-Outs isn't taken promptly and deliberately, Drop-Outs may assume they're leaving with the blessing or at least the permission of their church. If they feel the church wanted them to leave, Drop-Outs become almost impossibly hard-to-reach.

Missing Persons Report—Four Million of Them!

The magnitude of the church drop-out problem is staggering. Roughly 450 thousand members of United Methodism's 9.6 million members move from one city to another annually. That's a bit less than a 5 percent yearly mobility rate, not alarmingly high in mobile America.

The crunch comes when only about half of those 450 thousand mobile Methodists transfer their memberships to other Methodist congregations. The other half either switches denominations or simply drops out.[3]

Southern Baptist churches show slightly over 28 percent of all Southern Baptists are classified as nonresident members. In general, downtown congregations in large cities in the West and Midwest have the highest percentages of inactive members. In all, dropped-out Southern Baptists add up to roughly 4 million church members. For bragging purposes, we claim roughly 14 million Southern Baptists. In reality, our active membership is nearer 10 million. Obviously, 10 million is still a great host of members. But what about the 4 million Drop-Outs?

The Methodists and Southern Baptists aren't the only major denominations filing missing persons reports on their lapsed members. Roman Catholics report 12 million of their numbers are so alienated from the church as to be considered churchless.[4] In all, perhaps 100 million Americans are nominal or marginal church members. The trends are apparent. The overall number of members on church rolls is inflated. Drop-out church members need to be enlisted again but at a more profound level.

Whatever Became of What's-His-Name?

People drop out of church for a variety of reasons. Life disruptions, a loss of religious will, and church fights serve to illustrate the drop-out category.

Life Disruptions

Disruptions of life create the setting for most drop-out activity. Any number of life's changes can interrupt lifelong patterns of church participation.[5] The changes may relate both to natural stages in the human life cycle and to unexpected occurrences.

The young single. High school graduation is an important life passage. Collegians or career young adults are on their own. They finally have a chance to set their own schedules, choose their own friends, and select their life directions. This heady freedom often doesn't include church participation.

The empty nester. When all the children leave home, parents frequently drop out of church. Some parents have seen the church as providing religious education and moral values for their children. Others have anticipated the freedom to travel and to enjoy less family responsibility. In either event, the empty nest provides one occasion to drop out of church.

The mourner. One study of Drop-Outs indicates the experience of loss disrupts church members' participation.[6] Supportive persons have been lost. Spouses have begun jobs. Invalid parents have been taken back into children's homes. Each of these events can be experienced as loss, and one way to cope with the natural grief process is to stop going to church.

The ulcer culture. Some success-oriented persons immerse themselves in a pressurized life-style and relish it. Then stress or a health problem, such as an ulcer, begins to plague these high-octane overachievers. In an attempt to ease out from under some of their rigorous responsibilities, they jettison church activity and use the weekend to escape their work pressures.

Loss of Religious Will

Some congregational members feel their participation in the institutional church has drained them of the will to proceed spiritually. This feeling is experienced particularly by burned-out members and by the anti-institutionalists. Another category of Drop-Outs privatize their faith and avoid institutional church responsibilities.

The burned out. Russell Hale's study uncovered a sizable group of church people who felt they'd done their bit, paid their dues, and no longer wanted to be tied down. They felt tired, and some felt used and abused. In an attempt to travel lighter, burned-out members drop out of church activities. To illustrate, when asked to teach Sunday School for a twenty-sixth conservative year, a church member refused with, "I'm going to retire."

One burned-out church member reported to Hale: "To keep things going, the core workers, about thirty-five of us, had to do everything. You get bombarded. We felt guilty saying no. The church wanted all our time—and too much money. They felt we should do everything, and we weren't ready to do that. We're out now."[7]

The anti-institutionalists.—Some Drop-Outs have been close to former ministers and distanced themselves from their congregation when the minister left. One embittered member claimed, "I would probably be in the Christian church now had it not been they fired the best man I ever knew."[8]

The private church. Other Drop-Outs avoid corporate church activities. Using either a small group or religious television programs as a base, they aim at feeling good while remaining free of obligations. They are uncommitted to evangelism, missions, and ministry. The Drop-Out who aligns informally with the electronic church doesn't have to admit personal imperfections or be confronted with the shortcomings of the TV preacher either.

Conflicts in the Congregation

One of the outcomes of church fights is members may move to the fringes of the church and drop out. These church members retain membership on paper but stop participating in any constructive way. Several groups drop out due to conflict.

The defeated. Some Drop-Outs have taken sides in congregational disputes. They actively took part in the disagreements and were beaten—emotionally, by vote, or by rumor. Consequently, they've withdrawn in embarrassment or hostility.

The battle fatigued. These Drop-Outs haven't necessarily taken sides or debated congregational issues. But they've been worn down by the emotional wear and tear of the conflicts. They've simply tired of the dissension and dropped out to escape the emotional expenditure of conflict.

The blamed. Some members carry the stigma for church conflicts in which they have been relatively uninvolved. For example, they may innocently state their concern and discover their testimony is the "straw which breaks the camel's back." Or, they may have been "in charge" during an unfortunate episode of conflict and get blamed because the outcome is unsatisfactory. For instance, the chairperson of a pastor selection committee may receive blame if the pastor turns out to be immoral or a scoundrel.

A frightening trend toward private religion is emerging. Over 70 percent of both the churched and unchurched claim a believer can be a good Christian or Jew without attending church or synagogue. For these folk, religion is strictly a private affair. Believing is becoming divorced from belonging for an increasing number. Interestingly, most of those who have privatized their faith grew up in a traditional religious background. They aren't hostile toward congregations generally; they see no positive reason to align their lives with a worshiping and ministering fellowship.[9]

Recovering Drop-Outs

By and large, congregations have dropped their Drop-Outs. Only about one church in ten appears to be making any systematic effort to reactivate fringe members, according to our observations. When congregations don't try to reenlist their disengaged members, these hard-to-reach Drop-Outs feel completely excluded.[10]

What do Drop-Outs need relationally and theologically from

the church? Drop-Outs with disrupted life patterns have been thrown off balance; they need to assess their losses, grieve, and restore life's equilibrium. Those Drop-Outs who have lost their religious will feel worn; they want support and time to renew themselves. Persons who have dropped out because of conflict feel hurt, let down, or put down; they may be reinvolved if healing and reconciling initiatives are taken.

The theological and relational baseline for Drop-Outs is fellowship, *koinonia*. A variety of outreach strategies can be tailored to fit these relational and theological needs. Each strategy can use *koinonia* as its foundation.

Back from the Fringe

Whichever dynamic or concern serves as the occasion for dropping out, the initiative to reinvolve Drop-Outs depends on the congregation. Several outreach approaches can be used to reincorporate the Drop-Out into the life of the church.

Watch for Drop-Outs' Early Warning Signals

Drop-Outs usually signal their anxiety, anger, or disaffection before they actually fall away. Preliminary steps are taken by potential Drop-Outs to create some distance from leaders, groups, or the entire congregation. For example, a pastor-friend notes some Drop-Outs have hinted of their growing discomfort with him by changing their customary seating patterns and moving further away from him during worship services. They actually begin their withdrawal by trying to get more distance from their pastor—especially if he's the cause of their anger or the object of their anxiety. Such nonverbal signals may offer clues to potential Drop-Outs' mind-set. The strategy of the pastor mentioned above is to reduce distance by moving to the potential Drop-Outs with visits, concern, attention, and recognition.

Bill Schutz has outlined a cycle of group development which may give us eyes to see the church member who's considering dropping out.[11] Schutz claims new group members' normal concerns are first getting in, then becoming influential, and finally feeling cared for; the group development sequence, according to Schutz, is in-top-near. Unfortunately, groups can dissolve too. In that event, members first create distance, then rock the boat about who's in charge, and finally drop out; the group dissolution pattern is far-bottom-out.

Schutz asserts committed group members feel they belong, have influence, and are loved. If that commitment process is upset, they move away from the center of things, cause conflict, and eventually quit. Reversing the distancing process, then, is crucial to keeping alienated church members from joining the ranks of the Drop-Outs. Distance must be reduced by any appropriate ministry method.

Visit Drop-Outs as Early as Possible

Intuitively, we know Drop-Outs have experienced some anxiety, anger, hostility, or guilt. And we suspect we're going to inherit some of their negative feelings if we make a home visit on them. Expect some pain.

A Methodist pastor discovered a middle-aged couple who had become angry with him, but for four years he neglected calling on them. Finally, he phoned for an appointment and went to their home. He reported:

> It was a snowy, wintery day in Rochester, New York, when I pulled up to their home. We chatted about surface issues. Then the wife said to me, "You have not been here for four years. Why not?" The tone of her voice was hostile and the question was not one of inquiry but of hidden resentment. My response was, "I didn't know that people, who were once active in the church like you were, went through such severe pain in becoming inactive. I certainly was not sensitive to your cries for help, and I am sincerely sorry for my insensitivity. I hope you will forgive me." The woman began to cry. Her husband came and sat beside her on the couch and put his arm

around her. For the next two hours I sat and let them share the deep pain that was inside them because of leaving the church.

I happened to be the anxiety-provoking event in their leaving. In listening to them, they were able to share their hostility toward me around the issue that occurred nearly four years earlier. They related how they had lost the community in which they had found great comfort and love, and how they felt bad about the alienation with me personally but did not know how to go about bringing about reconciliation. They related how their children had been out of the church school and youth fellowship for that same period of time and that they felt inadequate as parents; and, finally, how, once they had left the church community, they did not know how to gracefully return, and therefore stayed on the outside. They had, in fact, cried for help to me through the Pastor-Parish Relations Committee, but at that time in my life I was not sensitive to the cries for help that people give prior to leaving. If I had been sensitive to that earlier, I would have saved a lot of pain for them and myself.[12]

None of us enjoys hearing the pain or receiving the anger of others. Their pain stirs our feelings—even our guilt and anger. But the cleansing which comes through shared pain is often necessary for healing and growth. Nothing is more pivotal to the Christian gospel, after all, than experiences of reconciliation.

So visit Drop-Outs early on. Brace for their pain. Listen. Feel with them. Try to understand. Pray and work for reconciliation.

Heighten Congregational Awareness of and Responsibility for Drop-Out Members

To let Drop-Outs go unretrieved runs the risk of extending the drop-out cycle further. That is, if the Drop-Outs have burned out from carrying a disproportionate part of their church's ministry load, the present burden for ministry has been shifted to a new generation of burnout candidates. Lacking the painful experience and wisdom of earlier Drop-Outs puts the current church leaders in jeopardy. In other words, those who have burned out may be the only members who know the warning symptoms of losing religious willpower.

Of course, another congregational dimension of prompt care of Drop-Outs involves the natural network of relationships in a healthy congregation. If an early attempt is made to recover Drop-Outs, there are more relational links to the Drop-Out. The longer a Drop-Out is away from the church fellowship, the less likely laypersons are to have opportunities for taking initiative for enlisting the Drop-Out again.

Try a Church-Member Revival

Revivals have traditionally been aimed at evangelizing the lost. Some congregations may need internal renewal before they can effectively reach out to the unsaved. Churches with a large number of Drop-Outs might consider a church-member revival as a preparatory step to evangelism.

How can a church renew its own members? Focus on strengthening the congregation's sense of fellowship. Develop a list of inactive members. Arrange a systematic visitation plan. Structure warm, informal worship services. Include a broad range of *koinonia*-developing elements during the revival—fellowships, meals, informal dialogues, children's sermons, and the like. Keep the focus on members covenanting together to serve Christ. And guard against making reaching Drop-Outs your church's major evangelism strategy. Non-Christians still must be reached while Drop-Outs are retrieved. Both keeping and reaching members is vital for congregational health.

Trying Is Succeeding

What constitutes success in reaching Drop-Outs? A 100 percent recovery rate is ideal but unrealistic. However, some Drop-Outs are recovered for productive service.

Take heart from these statistics. Almost half of all Americans (46 percent) drop out of active religious participation sometime during their lifetimes. Teens are most apt to drop out. That's the bad news. The good news is that 80 percent of religious Drop-Outs reinvolve themselves actively in congregations. Outreach leaders need to be sensitive to the ebb and flow of religious activity levels in others' lives; they also need to draw encouragement from the likelihood that many inactives respond to caring initiatives.[13]

John Mark, for example, abandoned Barnabas and Paul's first missionary journey (Acts 13:13). But Mark returned and served Christ effectively again. He became Barnabas's new partner in missionary work (Acts 15:39). Later Paul forgave Mark and included Mark in his circle of valued friends (Col. 4:10). And the final proof of Mark's recommitment is the Synoptic Gospel bearing his name. Mark's biography of Jesus, probably the eyewitness report of Simon Peter, briefly describes the vigor and excitement of Christ's life and ministry.

We'll not enjoy the slow, painful work of reaching out to Drop-Outs. We'll not retrieve them all. But the joy of recovering an occasional John Mark for productive service will make our efforts to touch the spectrum of local church Drop-Outs worthwhile. At the very least, healthy churches try to reinvolve their Drop-Out members. And trying yields some important successes along the way. Not all hard-to-reach Drop-Outs are unresponsive. Many will return to active service in local congregations.

Notes

1. John S. Savage, *The Apathetic and Bored Church Member: Psychological and Theological Implications* (Pittsford, N. Y.: LEAD Consultants, 1976), p. 97.

2. Richard D. Vangerud, "A Study of Certain Inactive Members in a Local Congregation," *Journal of Pastoral Care,* Mar. 1978, p. 17.

3. David E. Anderson, "Methodist Project Keeps Tabs on Mobile Membership," *Raleigh Times,* 11 Dec. 1982, p. 4-B.

4. Lewis Wingo, "Where Are All Those Nonresident Members?" *Quarterly Review*, Apr.-Mar.-June 1976, pp. 68-71. Projections suggest that the 4 million level has now been bypassed.

5. Lyle E. Schaller, *Hey, That's Our Church!* (Nashville: Abingdon, 1975), p. 17. Schaller notes three major occasions when church members drop out of their congregations: a move to a different community, when a person graduates from high school, and soon after the youngest child leaves the home nest.

6. Vangerud, pp. 7-20.

7. J. Russell Hale, *The Unchurched* (San Francisco: Harper and Row, 1980), p. 126.

8. Ibid, p. 114.

9. "The Unchurched American," *Grapevine*, 15 Jan. 1984, pp. 1-6. Religious Drop-Outs are a challenge to most communities of faith. For a Roman Catholic perspective, see Dean R. Hoge, et al, *Converts, Dropouts, Returnees: a Study of Religious Change Among Catholics* (New York: Pilgrim Press, 1981). For the viewpoint of Jewish scholars, see David Caplovitz and Fred Sherrow, *The Religious Drop-Outs: Apostasy among College Graduates* (Beverly Hills: Sage Publications, 1977). For a Mormon point of view, see John F. Seggar and Reed H. Blake, "Post-Joining Nonparticipation: an Exploratory Study of Convert Inactivity," *Review of Religious Research*, 11 (Spring 1970), pp. 204-209.

10. Hale, p. 41; Robert D. Dale, *To Dream Again* (Nashville: Broadman Press, 1981), p. 125.

11. William C. Schutz, *The Interpersonal Underworld* (Palo Alto, Calif.: Science and Behavior Books, 1966), p.

12. John Savage, "Pain Precedes Healing," *Ministry*, May 1981, p. 7.

13. David A. Roozen, "Church Dropouts: Changing Patterns of Disengagement and Re-entry," *Review of Religious Research*, 21 (Supplement 1980), pp. 427-450.

5
Case Studies of Evangelized Drop-Outs

We referred to several biblical cases of Drop-Outs at the beginning and end of chapter 4. Among those, John Mark and Simon Peter were reclaimed. Elsewhere the Bible says, "They went out from us, but they were not of us; for if they had been of us, they would have continued with us; but they went out, that it might be plain that they all are not of us" (1 John 2:19). We may never reclaim all Drop-Outs any more than the New Testament churches did. But we can reclaim some.

This chapter relates three contemporary cases where the persons were evangelized and returned to useful kingdom service and meaningful church membership. Each of these dropped out because of life's disruptions and not because of religious burnout or church fights. The case of John W. Collins, Jr., may also have been included in the Locked-Out category, especially so if it had ended with his initial conversion at age nineteen.

"The Black Sheep of the Family": The Case of John W. Collins, Jr.[1]

John was born in 1931 and born again in 1950 at the age of nineteen. John's parents were separated before he ever knew his mother. His father made moonshine whiskey, gambled, and drank heavily. The one bright spot in his early life was the tender love and care extended to him by his grandmother, uncles, and other relatives on his father's side of his extended family. They were all devout Christians.

"During those early years, I remember how I was badly

mistreated; always receiving a thrashing for things that did not make sense. There was no real love. I have a sister eighteen months younger than I, and it appeared as though she received the best of care and attention; being loved while I was pushed aside and was somewhat like the Black Sheep of the family.

"I cannot forget the abuse that I received and that feeling of hatred toward me. Throughout my young years, through all sorts of mistreatment, I was shuffled back and forth from Maryland to Virginia just to get me out of the way. I was thrown off on my aunt and uncle, and my grandmother. Because of this type of treatment and while growing up, I developed a very nervous complex which left its mark even to this day."

At fourteen, John quit school and became self-supporting. "I became a hardened person, and fighting was my middle name." He joined the U. S. Army at fifteen, having lied about his age and with his father's assistance.

The sixteen-year-old soldier was stationed in Tokyo. He became a boxer, started drinking heavily, and associated with bad company. While drunk, two of his buddies went on a rampage of crime, taking him along while passed out in the backseat of a taxi. The ringleader got a three-year sentence, the lesser involved soldier four years, and John received a five-year prison sentence! His time was reduced because of good behavior, and he was paroled into his father's custody in 1949.

When John visited his father's people, he attended the Cambria Baptist Church in Cambria, Virginia. They incarnated God's love for him. His grandmother Collins had given him a Bible before he went to Japan. That Bible became important to him while he was in prison. He even began to attend the prison chapel. Inevitably, not long after he was paroled, John was back in Cambria with those who loved him so dearly.

"In early 1950, my grandmother (my mother's mother) died in my arms. It was then that I had my first real encounter with the Lord. I'll never forget that night as she lay dying. I peered out the window toward an embankment which was several yards away. It was a moonless night, pitch dark, and suddenly, I saw a white figure of a person and this figure was much like a cloud, yet there was no face to be seen. I felt the need to grow closer to God to find an explanation of this experience. Shortly afterwards, I accepted Christ as my personal Lord and Savior at Cambria Baptist Church where all the family were members, and was baptized into the fellowship on April 30, 1950."

A month later, the Korean War began. The baby Christian again lied about his past, enlisted in the Army Reserve, and was soon off to Korea for twenty-two months. He returned to the States with battle fatigue and a nervous breakdown. All of his past was confessed to the army, which forgave him but not without an undesirable discharge.

God didn't have much of a conscious place in John's life from 1950 until late 1976 when John tried to commit suicide. He married, became the father of a daughter and a son, excelled in his work and business, became addicted to alcohol, had major surgery several times, almost died from an ulcer and its complications, had problems communicating with his wife and children, lost his father to death in 1973, briefly tried Alcoholics Anonymous, had several strokes, and became addicted to his medication. In general, he went from bad to worse, and finally hit bottom.

Along the way on John's toboggan trail, after the first few years, God did send one of His messengers to John. "There was a fellow worker who continually observed my conduct and saw my life being wasted. He was a very active Christian, and every opportunity he had, he would read Scripture. Then one day he approached me and asked me if I knew the Lord Jesus. I answered 'Yes.' Then he knew that I was in a backslidden condition. Finally, he convinced me to attend the Overlea Baptist Church. Again, I wanted to straighten my life out, and my wife was eager to see me do so. So we attended church about three different times. However, I continued to drink and run around, not caring one way or another. Then, knowing what I was doing and knowing that I was wrong, I promised myself that I would never attend church again until *I* was ready to really accept it; to do the work of the Lord."

John did things *his* way. He saw no way out of the mess he had made. Desperately, he sought help on the telephone: from the hospital, the police, a "hot line" for troubled people. No help was given. So he slashed one of his wrists with a razor, severing everything.

On December 5, 1976, while recovering from his death attempt in the Phipps Clinic, John experienced another epiphany. "All through the night, I paced the floors as my whole life passed before my eyes. I was thanking God again and again for sparing my life. I would lay down for a little while, then pace the floor, and so on. Then about 6:00 that early Sunday morning, I was overcome with sleepiness and lay down on my bed. I fell into a deep sleep and had this strange vision or dream. I was living during the time of the apostle Paul in Philippi. I did not see him, but knew about him, and all around me were Roman soldiers. Suddenly at 7:00 that morning, exactly one hour later, I was awakened by a brilliant stream of light, so brilliant that it was blinding to me. It was frightening. Then I heard a voice speaking to me and I knew that it was Jesus as He said, 'John it is all over now, you must follow me. Come!' "

Out of the depths of despair and through that dark valley

of shadows, John turned back to God and to the church. He called a faithful Southern Baptist pastor who came to his aid and lovingly guided him back into the light.

Today, John is no longer the black sheep of his family or the family of God, the church. The Lord is his Shepherd, and he plans to "dwell in the house of the LORD for ever" (Ps. 23:6).

Commentary on "The Black Sheep of the Family"

John was caught up in a drop-out syndrome. As a boy, he was dropped in and out of his father's home and the homes of his relatives in Virginia. At fourteen he dropped out of school. At fifteen he dropped out of home and community into the U. S. Army. At sixteen he was dropped out of the military service into a five-year prison sentence. At seventeen he was dropped out of prison into parole. At nineteen he dropped out of the church and out of civilian life back into the U. S. Army. At about twenty-one he was dropped out of the military a second time.

His whole life script, almost from the day he was born, had "Drop-Out" written across it. The suicide attempt was intended to be his ultimate drop-out, the final denouement.

Dropping out was John's way of coping, his method of survival, an escape mechanism from harsh realities. Life's disruptions swept him about like plankton in the sea. He was never, until 1976, all the way into any institution—not his parental family, his father's family, the U. S. Army, any job he held, any hospital which treated him, or any other institution including the church. We do not marvel that he became a Drop-Out from the church because he was never fully into it. Formally and technically, yes, but never fully assimilated because he was a rootless nomad.[2]

Multiple forces pulled John into the church when he first got right with God. He read the Bible given him by his Grandmother Collins and even attended the Cambria Baptist Church while visiting his father's people. Probably the strongest magnet pulling John into the church was the forever love of his father's family. Their steadfast love has in fact nurtured and sustained him to this day. But the immediate push which drove the young parolee into the arms of Jesus was the vision he had that night in 1950 when his other grandmother died in his arms.

Visions played a significant role in John's life. The two greatest turning points in his pilgrimage center around the two visions of 1950 and 1976. Those visions were epiphanies through which God came to John and made His will known. Note the contrast between the metaphors of darkness and light and death and life in the visions.

Some persons seem so structured because of the ways in which they have experienced life that nothing short of a vision or dream in which God Himself appears to them will suffice. That could account in part for the inability of John's fellow worker to get through to John when he got John to attend Overlea Baptist Church. No human being, in fact, be he or she a wife, son, daughter, pastor, doctor, or whatever, seemed able to get John's full attention from 1950 to 1976.

Everything was downhill from about mid-fifties until late 1976. John called himself a black sheep. And so he was, for that is a scapegrace or an incorrigible rascal. He became a black sheep of the family of God as well as of his flesh-and-blood family.

Even God didn't get John's full attention until the suicide attempt. Nevertheless, that does not put down the importance of human witnesses in the evangelization of Drop-Outs. John's visions did mysteriously move him into the orbit of faith, but more than fleeting visions are required for a Christian to grow in Christlike character and conduct. God also appeared to John in the human form of a faithful pastor who patiently guided him back into the light. Furthermore, would anyone discount the enfleshment of the gospel by significant others throughout John's Abrahamic journey?

"No One Could Tell by Our Life-Style": The Case of Hollis E. Johnson, III[3]

"As a nine-year-old boy, I came to know Jesus through the witness of a Southern Baptist church and a Christian home. I spent many hours around the church, and the members were in and out of our home as a result of the active participation of my mother and father in the work of the church. I can still remember talking to my pastor, mother, and father in our living room prior to making my public commitment and subsequent baptism.

"Following my profession of faith in our Lord, I was active in Sunday School, Youth Week, and became an usher as a teenager. Then in my mid-teens, I became more interested in the materialism of this world and less active in church. My grades suffered, my commitment to things of real substance waned, and my relationship with my family became merely perfunctory because I knew more than they or, for that matter, God.

"The drifting continued through college and service in the navy. When I embarked on my career in banking, I used the same old yardsticks: salary, friends, position, prestige, and worldly recognition. My wife, Celeste, and I only attended Sunday morning worship services, and then only when it was convenient. No one could tell by our life-style that we knew the Savior.

"The Holy Spirit began to work on us, but we continued to resist. It took tragedy for Him to get our attention. We had to face the loss of two babies, one prior to birth and the other forty-eight minutes after birth, without leaning on the Comforter. It was at this point of despair that we finally realized what was missing in our lives: a personal relationship with and dependence on Jesus Christ.

"Further, we were denying our children the experience of

learning about Him through the fellowship of His church. We finally prayed: Lord, we cannot do it on our own, we need You, and we are going to turn it all over to You. What a relief!

"We started back to Sunday School at my home church, Belmont Heights, in Nashville, as difficult as it was. Thank God, the church welcomed us back like the father welcomed his prodigal son, and we became active in the total program.

"As we began to grow spiritually, we began to seek God's will for our lives. Bill Stephens, Sunday School teacher, and my Sunday School class were a great help and support during this time. Then the Spirit started making me unhappy with my job as vice president and trust officer and manager of the investment management division of Nashville's largest bank. It just wasn't fun anymore.

"One of our accounts which I handled was the Southern Baptist Foundation, and I met monthly with the Executive Committee. When Kendall Berry retired as executive secretary, the Foundation directors turned to me. Their offer and my awareness of my dissatisfaction with my work where I was coincided to such an extent that it had to be God's will. All that prayer had been answered by the offering of this particular place of service where my work experience could be used for God's glory. What a tremendous thrill to experience this kind of walk with God.

"After four years here, I find there are still problems and difficulties. All operations have them. But since I am attempting to depend on God who created me and gave me what talents I have, I find the work is exciting, challenging, and joyous, and I look forward to each new day."

Commentary on "No One Could Tell by Our Life-Style"

The case assumes others should be able to tell by our life-styles that we are Christians. The Drop-Out life-style described here is characterized by materialism, perfunctory family relationships, drifting, and measuring one's success by such yardsticks as salary, friends, position, prestige, and worldly recognition. Furthermore, these Drop-Outs "only attended Sunday morning worship services, and then only when it was convenient."

Hollis and Celeste were *in* the church but not really a part *of* it. They once had a meaningful relationship with Christ, but at a point of despair they realized what was missing in their lives: "a personal relationship with and dependence on Jesus Christ."

Life-style may be a big point to consider in trying to evangelize Drop-Outs, both their life-style and ours.[4] We dare not assume persons are practicing Christians merely because they have some formal relationship with a church.

How did this couple become aware of their Drop-Out life-style? Hollis had been exposed to a Christian life-style in his parents' home and in Belmont Heights Baptist Church. He had professed his faith in Christ at age nine and been active in church work until his mid-teens.

The Holy Spirit began to work on Hollis and his wife. "It took a tragedy for Him to get our attention," said Hollis. "We had to face the loss of two babies, one prior to and the other forty-eight minutes after birth, without leaning on the Comforter." The couple also began to realize they were denying their children the experience of learning about Christ through the fellowship of the church.

Hollis did not forsake the assembly because of a big church fight. Like so many other Drop-Outs, he left in his mid-teens. The drifting continued through college and a hitch in the navy, into marriage, parenthood, and a banking career. Progressively he moved farther and farther from the church until the tragedy with his babies. That kind of pattern may be seen again and again in the reclamation of some Drop-Outs.

It was difficult for Hollis and Celeste to admit they couldn't fill what was missing in their life-style on their own. But Belmont Church made it easier for them. Does your church welcome Drop-Outs like the father welcomed the prodigal son back home?

With the help of a Sunday School teacher and others, Hollis began to grow spiritually and to seek God's will for his life. Today he is using his training and gifts to head the Southern Baptist Foundation in Nashville. Drop-Outs can be evangelized. Frequently, when they are reclaimed, they become very useful servants of Christ.

"Sexually Abused and Violently Battered": The Case of Anne-Marie Kidwell[5]

"Although my parents, school, and church instilled in me a deep love for God, I did not have a saving knowledge of the Messiah until later in life. For twenty-eight years of my life, I suffered from abuse of one kind or another. After being sexually abused as a child and violently battered as a wife, I lost all sense of personal worth. I began to abuse myself with alcohol, drugs, sexual immorality, and an attempt to end my life. Satan had made every effort to destroy me and was well on the way to success, but God did not have that in His plan. He had His hand on my life even while I was being destroyed by my sin.

"One day someone told me about Jesus Christ and His power to heal broken lives. By the grace of God, I was healed of a heroin addiction, but I did not give my life over totally to the Lord. I read the Bible with a consummate passion, but I did not realize that knowledge about the Bible could not get me into heaven. I believed in my *head* and confessed with my mouth that Jesus Christ was the Son of God and had died for the sins of the world, but I had never accepted it into my heart. I read about the fruit of the Spirit in Galatians 5:22-23 and wondered why it was not evident in my own life, then Satan began to tempt me. He would tell me that my sins had not been forgiven because they were unforgivable. He didn't just rob me of my faith but was well on the way of possessing even my desire to believe. I began wallowing around in the mire of self-pity, but still the Lord had His hand on me.

"The Lord used an incident during the delivery of my little daughter to make Himself an undeniable reality in my life. I had gone into surgery for a cesarean section to deliver my baby. For some reason, unknown to me, the anesthesia did not take effect; the surgeon began operating and delivered my baby while I was conscious. I lay helplessly on the table unable to utter a sound. My inner being cried out to the Lord, and He answered me. My life has not been the same since that moment. I have encountered my Savior in a real and personal way. Two weeks later, I recommitted my life in a church service, but in retrospect I realize that I was born again at that time.

"My desire to pray, spread the good news, and just love those around me in the same way which He loved me became insatiable. A short time later, the Lord led me to Kansas City and Bales Baptist Church. I was baptized in this church on October 19, 1980. Since I have been a member of Bales, the Lord has been speaking to my heart and leading me into ministry. He told me that He would guide me into the streets to bring the Word to the people. He told me that although pain had sought to destroy me, He did not allow it to happen. He had allowed me to suffer so that I would have compassion. He told me that if I would read His Word and pray and reach out to those who need Him in obedience to His command, He would touch them and heal them.

"Although I feel unworthy to be used in the way in which

God has called me, I look to the Cross and realize that I have no choice but to obey. I am compelled to evangelize: to pray for, witness to, win, and disciple souls. I must answer yes to His call to go and make disciples (Matt. 28:19). As Paul said, 'If I preach the gospel, I have nothing to boast of, for I am under compulsion; for woe is me if I do not preach the gospel' (1 Cor. 9:16, NASB).

"I must proclaim the gospel of Christ—the Living Hope— to the terminal generation, or I will die."

Commentary on "Sexually Abused and Violently Battered"

There are several striking features in this case. Anne-Marie's sense of personal worth was correlated with her spiritual formation. She was sexually abused as a child and violently battered as a wife. Having been treated as worthless, she lost all sense of personal worth and began to abuse and batter herself. Little wonder that one who was "dropped" on so violently for so long should drop out of society and the church so completely!

But look what happened when she regained her self-worth. She desired to love those around her as God had loved her. She saw herself as one chosen to minister to persons like she had been and to evangelize the "terminal generation." Her self-image changed and improved as she gained more knowledge of God's power and love.

Any strategy for reaching Drop-Outs like Anne-Marie should seek to improve their self-image. We can tell the Anne-Maries of our communities about the power of God to heal and help through sharing our testimonies and our life stories.[6] We can demonstrate God's love for them through friendship evangelism.[7]

One unusual feature in the case is that Anne-Marie apparently dropped out of the church twice. Initially her parents, school, and church instilled in her a deep love for God. That one did not take because she "did not have a saving knowledge of the Messiah until later in life." Next, she was told about Jesus Christ and His power to heal broken lives. At that time, she was healed of a heroin addiction but did not give her life over totally to the Lord.

False starts in one's journey toward the city of God can produce spiritual stillbirths. This case shows us how important it is for Christian witnesses to lead new converts to believe in their hearts as well as in their heads. "I did not realize that knowledge about the Bible could not get me into heaven," said Anne-Marie. Our objective should not be to get persons to give mere mental assent to a set of facts about Jesus Christ but to trust their whole life to His care and direction. A complete approach to evangelizing Drop-Outs should begin at the front end of conversion and initiation into the church.

Anne-Marie was conscious of some kind of warfare going on in her life. In her mind, Satan and God were set against each other in the battle for her soul. At one point, following her head trip toward Christ, Satan tried to tell her that her sins were "unforgivable." The congregation which desires to evangelize Drop-Outs should be aware of the power encounter going on in some of their minds between the forces of light and darkness. Some Drop-Outs actually think they have committed the unpardonable sin of blasphemy against the Holy Spirit (see Mark 3:28-30).

This case presents us with several significant turnings in the battered young lady's life. She turned first to the church. Frequently, persons brought up in Christian homes and churches turn to the church before they turn to Christ. Next, she turned to the Bible, which could not get her into heaven but did bear witness to Jesus Christ. Then, when her baby was born, she turned to Christ and was born again. Finally, she turned to the Christian world mission with a compulsion to share the gospel in the streets. The case is unclear as to when, or if, she turned to the Christian ethic.

In building a strategy to evangelize hard-to-reach Drop-Outs, we should remember that evangelizing happens when the receiver (the potential disciple) turns to Christ, to the Christian message and ethic, to a Christian congregation, and to the world in love and mission—*in any order*. Those of us committed to the ideal of a regenerate church membership composed of believers only would, of course, prefer that the first turning be to Christ. An intelligent and wholesome evangelism, however, does require all four turnings in order to be complete.[8]

God used many witnesses to reach Anne-Marie: parents, school, church, Bible, and a cesarean section in which the anesthesia did not take effect. But let us not overlook that witness who one day told her about Jesus Christ and His power to heal broken lives. If we Christians don't tell the Anne-Maries about Jesus Christ and His power to heal, who will?

Notes

1. Those parts of this case in quotation marks were written by Rev. John W. Collins, Jr., who graduated from Southeastern Baptist Theological Seminary in 1981. The remainder is based on Mr. Collins's unpublished autobiography and testimony. All of it is used with his permission.

2. For information on the process of reaching and assimilating new members into the church, we recommend Lyle E. Schaller, *Assimilating New Members* (Nashville: Abingdon, 1978).

3. This case was written by Hollis E. Johnson, III and originally appeared in *The Baptist Program*, May 1981, pp. 10 & 11. It is used with permission.

4. We recommend the following books on life-style evangelism: C. B. Hogue, *Love Leaves No Choice: Life-Style Evangelism* (Waco, Texas: Word Books, Publisher, 1976); Jim Petersen, *Evangelism as a Lifestyle* (Colorado Springs: Navpress, 1980); and Joseph C. Aldrich, *Life-Style Evangelism* (Portland: Multnomah Press, 1981).

5. This case was written by Anne-Marie Kidwell, age twenty-eight, in March 1981 and is used with her permission. The name is fictitious, but

the facts were attested by Rev. David Baker when he was pastor of Bales Baptist Church in Kansas City, Missouri, the church of which Anne-Marie was a member.

6. For help on organizing and sharing your personal testimony or life story, see Delos Miles, *Introduction to Evangelism*, pp. 161-185.

7. We recommend the following books on friendship evangelism: Arthur G. McPhee, *Friendship Evangelism: the Caring Way to Share Your Faith* (Grand Rapids: Zondervan Publishing House, 1978); Wayne McDill, *Making Friends for Christ* (Nashville: Broadman Press, 1979); Matthew Prince, *Winning Through Caring: Handbook on Friendship Evangelism* (Grand Rapids: Baker Book House, 1981); and Duncan McIntosh, *The Everyday Evangelist* (Valley Forge: Judson Press, 1984).

8. For a fuller discussion of these turnings, see George G. Hunter, III, *The Contagious Congregation: Frontiers in Evangelism and Church Growth* (Nashville: Abingdon, 1979), pp. 30-31.

6
The Locked-Outs: Removing Stigmas

Locked-Outs carry a stigma; they have been overtly rejected by churches. Consequently, the Locked-Outs have little interest in a congregation. The woman at the well in John 4 and Zacchaeus in Luke 19 are biblical examples of Locked-Outs. The woman at the well had adopted a sexual life-style which was unacceptable to traditional religion. Zacchaeus was a political turncoat and a cheat who was probably excluded from the synagogue. Locked out. They knew the religious institutions of their day were closed to them.

The Locked-Outs are persons whose life-styles are seen as deviant in some way. As such, they are shut away from the mainstream concerns and ministries of most congregations. Prisoners, addicts, sexual deviants, and ethnic minorities are generally in the locked-out category.

Who Gets Locked Out?

Hard-to-reach Americans who are potential Locked-Outs include:
- Persons who are known to have been admitted to mental institutions or drug and alcohol treatment centers
- Prisoners and ex-convicts
- Sexual deviants—homosexuals, bisexuals, transsexuals, and swingers
- Ethnic and racial groups
- Street addicts to drugs or alcohol
- Unmarried persons who are living together

- Celebrities
- The very rich, the up-and-outs
- Divorcees and remarrieds
- Nudists
- Single parents
- Couples in or children of interracial marriages.

The Locked-Outs, then, are a mixed bag of various subgroups who are hard-to-reach because of their life-styles.

Classifying the Locked-Outs

The Locked-Outs can be classified according to the aspect of their life-styles which makes them different from the mainstream church member. The Locked-Outs subdivide into the Lawbreakers, Standard Flaunters, Starting Overs, and persons in Different Molds.

Lawbreakers

Some Americans run afoul of our legal structures. Persons with arrest or prison records often become Locked-Outs.

The ex-prisoner. In America's early history, corporal and capital punishment were customary. In 1790, a new approach was developed in Philadelphia—prison. Even the term used for this more humane institution, *penitentiary,* implied prison was a place to be penitent—to work and study the Bible.

Today America ranks third in the world behind South Africa (400) and Russia (391) with 250 citizens out of every 100,000 population locked up. The United States operates over 6,500 penal institutions incarcerating over 500 thousand Americans on any given day. When an American has served his median sentence of 21 months and returns to free society, he may find some assistance at rescue missions or the Salvation Army.[1] Traditional churches show little concern however.

When the national picture is reduced to the state level, the prisoner's situation isn't any more comforting. For example, our state of North Carolina has 16,300 prisoners. When parolees and persons on probation are added to prisoners, the North Carolina Department of Corrections supervises one person out of every one hundred citizens. What are the statistics for your state? In spite of the magnitude of ex-prisoner audiences, few Christians minister inside jails regularly and few churches establish halfway houses or other outreach ministries. The ex-convict is essentially a Locked-Out. It's more the exception than the rule when a modern church announces "release to the captives" (Luke 4:18). Ex-prisoners are hard-to-reach for most congregations.

A few churches extend their ministries behind walls. One Tennessee church sponsors a Sunday School class at the Women's Prison in Nashville. When Sunday School attendance is announced, the minister typically reports, "We had four hundred in Bible study today and twenty-five more at the prison." A new member once drew a wrong assumption and shyly asked the pastor, "Exactly how many members do we have in prison?"

An association of churches in Asheville, North Carolina, has launched a ministry to prisoners' families. A Christian woman discovered only one chaplain served the prisoners in eight penal institutions for the twenty-two westernmost North Carolina counties. She acted as a catalyst to establish a cluster of seventy-five volunteers who witness to inmates and befriend the families of prisoners. This group hopes to develop a halfway house for former inmates soon. This Christian group is effectively evangelizing hard-to-reach persons who have run afoul of the law.

The live-ins. In many states, cohabitation is illegal. Nobody is quite sure how many Americans are currently living together unmarried or whether this trend is growing or waning. But this life-style isn't one many churches are comfortable with. Live-ins too, therefore, become Locked-Outs where the church is concerned.

The Standard Flaunters

Every society develops norms. Over a period of time, it becomes clear what's norm-al and what's ab-norm-al. Some citizens' life-styles confront social standards. These Standard Flaunters usually are Locked-Outs.

The addict. Addictions show up in a variety of guises. Some Americans eat too much, work too much, drink too much, or use prescription medications too much. Chemical abuse, or alcoholism and drug addiction, is affecting an increasing number of Americans. Tragically, both alcoholism and drug abuse are entangling younger persons all the time. For instance, national alcohol statistics now include a category for preteens. Addicts are prime candidates to become Locked-Outs.

Several years ago, I asked a youth group in an Arkansas church, "Do you have any alcoholics in this church?" "No," they answered with puzzlement.

"Do you have any drug addicts in this church?" "No," they replied firmly.

"Do you have any prostitutes in this church?" "No," they answered back almost indignantly.

The implication of my questions and their answers demonstrated a point. That congregation virtually required its members to be middle-class and moral prior to being invited to become Christians (shades of Acts 15 and the Jerusalem conference!) Their prospect list didn't include hard-to-reach persons like Locked-Outs.

The rich and famous. Celebrities can be Locked-Outs too. One Nashville, Tennessee, church has a legendary country music singer in its membership. He arrives late for worship and leaves before the benediction to keep from being hounded. He must face Sundays when he's tempted not to go to church just to avoid his personal and professional notoriety.

Ten percent of American households have an annual income exceeding fifty thousand dollars. A recent marketing survey divided the rich into five groupings. The Well-Feathered Nests are households with at least one high-income earner and children in the home. These families tend to be well educated but aren't apt to pursue luxury. The No-Strings-Attached household has at least one high-income earner and no children. Two thirds of this category exceeds 100 thousand dollars in yearly income. The Nanny's-in-Charge family has two or more breadwinners and children in the home. They are likely to involve themselves in sports activities and family outings. The Two-Career household is made up of two breadwinners and no children. The Good-Life household has no one employed and is usually comprised of affluent retirees.[2]

Novelist F. Scott Fitzgerald claimed the rich are different from you and me. Maybe. Our experience with affluent and wealthy Christians suggests two demands. First, they want quality in faith and in life. Second, they appreciate simplicity in the presentation of the gospel. In other words, rich hard-to-reach persons like both style and substance.

Rich or famous persons who are Christians have an important stewardship of influence. They can witness to and have an impact on other influential persons in ways the ordinary, man-on-the-street Christian sometimes can't.

The Starting-Overs

Some Locked-Outs haven't broken any laws or flaunted social conventions. But their lives bear the scars of bad judgment or rugged circumstances. They've had experiences which force them to start some dimensions of their lives over anew. Starting over may lock them out of some churches.

The formerly married. Whether just divorced or both divorced and remarried, a marital failure excludes many persons from comfortable church involvement. Family stability is a national problem. During 1980, 2.1 million American couples married; 1.1 million couples divorced during the same time frame.[3] One friend whose wife left him told me his church systematically locked him out.

Although he was a lifelong member of his congregation and had been Sunday School director and a deacon, he was informed immediately and directly that there was no place in that church for him as a divorcee. In another Baptist congregation, however, he found a meaningful ministry helping other formerly marrieds put their lives back together.

Churches as a rule aren't very comfortable reaching out to formerly marrieds. One Baptist divorcee, bitter over being excluded from her church, said: "I should have killed him. Baptists know how to deal with murder!" One fact is clear. There are few sympathy cards, supportive friends, or warm casseroles when the grief observed is a dead marriage.

The single parents. Trying to raise a family alone can become an overwhelming task. Whether the death of one's spouse or divorce creates a one-parent home, the range of roles and responsibilities is immense. And the extent of this family style is increasing. Single-parent and individual households are projected to increase from 53 percent of all American families to 57 percent by 1990.[4] Most churches are more oriented to couples than to singles. Some are so totally geared to nuclear families that single parents are among the Locked-Outs and become hard-to-reach.

The Different Molds

Some Locked-Outs are excluded because they simply don't fit. When viewed through certain congregations' filters, particular persons or groups are Locked-Outs because they are different in racial or ethnic background or in sexual preference. These Locked-Outs have been cast in Different Molds.

The ethnics. Race or ethnic background isn't a legal reason to exclude persons from employment or public accomodations. But congregations aren't technically bound by these laws. And some churches, either by atmosphere or voted policy, exclude racial and ethnic groups who differ from their primary group.

Southern Baptists are generally WASP (White Anglo-Saxon

Protestants) in makeup. But Blacks have become Southern Baptists' largest ethnic minority constituency. About 3500, or slightly less than one tenth, of Southern Baptist congregations report Black members, a total 275 thousand persons. About 50 thousand Blacks belong to predominantly white churches; Black Southern Baptist churches are mostly dually aligned with one of the National Baptist conventions. One hundred and fifty thousand Hispanics comprise Southern Baptist's second largest ethnic constituency.[4] Although some change is occurring, Southern Baptists remain predominantly European in ethnic background.

The sexual deviant. A variety of sexual life-styles is becoming more visible in our country. Homosexuality, bisexuality, transsexuality, and swinging are publicly discussed and displayed. The statistics for sexual deviancy are difficult to document, but America's homosexual population is estimated at 2 to 4 percent for males and 1 to 2 percent for females. The sexual deviant's life-style is so foreign to mainstream congregations' morality that proclamation and witness may be more likely than ministry and dialogue. While recent studies suggest Americans are becoming more traditional and conservative in their sexual behaviors, those persons whose life-styles deviate from the sexual norms fall into the hard-to-reach category.

Keys to the Locked-Outs

In general, Locked-Outs' life-styles awaken feelings of self-judgment and failure. Christians who know confession of sin opens the door to salvation can see the evangelistic potential of feelings of failure. A sense of shortcoming can open the door to experiences of healing and wholeness.

What do the Locked-Outs need from God and from us Christians? The Lawbreakers are excluded from the fellowship of many churches by their legal record. Feeling the condemnation of the law, Lawbreakers need divine and human forgiveness. Standard Flaunters feel they are set apart from the general population; they are exceptions in their own view. Feeling extraordinary and different, they need inclusion by accepting persons and groups. The Starting Overs are excluded from some traditional congregations by events of loss—death or divorce. They feel they've failed in relationships and need to be included and incorporated into a supportive community. Those from Different Molds sense they march to the beat of a different drummer. Their life-styles aren't customary when compared to most church members. Trying to understand the Different Molds is the key to ministering to persons who carry the stigma of estrangement. The basic themes of the gospel are keys to reaching Locked-Outs for Christ and the church.

Opening Up to the Locked-Outs

A range of evangelism and ministry strategies are suggested by Locked-Outs' basic needs. Healthy churches will focus on opening their ranks to persons who have been stigmatized and locked out by their life-styles.

Make a "Life-style Index"

As a church leader, try an experiment. For one week, read your local newspaper and watch your evening news. As news items are presented, ask yourself: Are the persons in these stories excluded from my church by life-style or events? Write down types of excluded persons or groups. Many of these folks will fit into the Locked-Out category. They may be persons you hadn't even considered inviting to church. As many as 90 percent of the persons listed on your life-style index may be Locked-Out because subconsciously they don't appear to mesh with your church. In a few cases, you may find Locked-Outs who have been intentionally kept on the outside. Your life-style index will help you identify and begin reaching out to the Locked-Outs of your community.

Areas Where No One Is Ministering

Watch for vacuum areas where no one is ministering. This approach fits the Locked-Out category well. To illustrate, consider a church in Nashville, Tennessee. Located in a neighborhood changing from single family homes to apartments and town houses, this congregation began having large numbers of formerly marrieds—many of them young divorced women with small children—visit the worship services. The pastor approached the deacons about trying a weekly discussion-and-support group for these formerly married adults. The deacons gave their permission but little support. The first group meeting drew six formerly marrieds. Within a year, the formerly married group was averaging eighty persons, many of whom became productive participants in the broader life of the congregation. In fact, the church became such a model in ministry to formerly marrieds that a half dozen other churches in the area sent representatives to the group meetings to observe and be trained.

The success of the Nashville church's formerly married ministry was rooted in a need no one else was attempting to meet. Ministry vacuums provide fertile seedbeds for evangelizing Locked-Outs and other hard-to-reach groups. When people hurt, they are apt to respond to the first offer of help—religious or secular. As the Civil War general discovered, success and effectiveness often goes to the group that's "fustest with the mostest."

One unique outreach ministry has been launched by a Texas church. This Methodist congregation in Fort Worth provides a worship service for severe allergy victims. Chronic allergy sufferers—persons who react strongly to perfume, dust, hair spray, after-shave lotion, cigarette smoke, and similar smells—end up ostracized from society. When confronted with the most extreme physical reactions to their ailment, these persons isolate themselves from friends, co-workers, and church gatherings. The Texas church provides an uncarpeted solarium with chairs separated by generous spacing. Hymn lyrics are printed on posters. Everyone, including the minister, follows strict rules about wearing or bringing anything that might set off an allergic reaction. The responses? Persons who had quit church because of their illness are enthusiastically attending these special services. One pleased participant reported, "When something is taken from you, it's very exciting to get it back again."[6] Without such a special effort, many of these hard-to-reach persons would likely miss out on Christian fellowship and perhaps the gospel itself.

Link with Other Helping Groups

Resource agencies who work with ex-prisoners or alcoholics or addicts have experience in the field. Consult with them for do's and don't's in working with special groups of Locked-Outs. They can help you get an effective ministry started and, in some instances, provide valuable training.

Use Ex-Locked-Outs to Minister

Use ex-Locked Outs to minister to other Locked-Outs. This principle has been a basic approach in such groups as Alcoholics Anonymous. Ex-addicts know from experience how drug users think and behave. Most important, they know how other Locked-Outs can be reached with the gospel.

Other Locked-Outs Changing the Locks

Reaching Locked-Outs calls for change. We know Christ can remake the life shattered by sin or tragedy. That's the unchanging good news of the gospel.

But some changes will also have to be made in congregations' attitudes and programs. That may be harder news to hear. In some cases, new information is needed in order to understand and help alcoholics and others. Anything new requires change, adjustment, and growth. And change is painful.

Churches may also have to surrender some stances they have

long held. For example, divorcees and Mexicans joining good ol' boys and Southern belles in worship won't cause the church building to fall down. In other words, the Locked-Outs may not be the threat to church and society we've made them out to be. One historic fact is clear. If, for example, prisoners were to be excluded from church involvement by God's mandate, Paul and most of the other apostles, and many of the early Baptists in Europe and America, would have been Locked-Outs.

Notes

1. These statistics are published in "Alternatives to Imprisonment," a Light and Leaven series pamphlet available from the Council on Christian Life and Public Affairs, P. O. Box 26508, Raleigh, NC 27611.

2. Robert Garfield, "The Rich: a Hard Group to Categorize," *USA Today*, 24 Oct. 1983, p. 3B.

3. Darryl J. Ellis and Peter P. Pekar, Jr., *Planning for Nonplanners* (New York: AMACOM, 1980), pp. 133-146.

4. Ibid.

5. "Blacks Said SBC Largest Minority," *Baptist and Reflector*, 6 May 1981, p. 3.

6. Jim Jones, "Texas Church Offers Worship Services for Allergy Victims," *Baptist Messenger*, 19 Jan. 1984, p. 13.

7
Case Studies of Evangelized Locked-Outs

Chapter 6 mentioned two biblical cases of evangelized Locked-Outs, the woman at the well (John 4:4-42) and Zacchaeus (Luke 19:1-10). Other biblical cases which fit here are: Legion (Mark 5:1-20); the Canaanite woman (Matt. 15:21-28); the two thieves (Luke 23:32-43); a woman caught in adultery (John 8:2-11); and a woman in the house of Simon (Luke 7:31-50).[1] This chapter highlights three contemporary cases, two single men and an ethnic widow.

"Too Much Emotional Pain": The Case of Chris Swalley[2]

"I was converted when I was thirty-one years of age. From the time I can remember, I've thought there most likely was some kind of a God. My experience with life before my conversion would not let me see God as a real person. My conversion experience has been a driving force of inspiration that He is a real person.

"I was sitting on a jail cell bunk in the Virginia Beach City Jail. I'll never forget the cold and empty feeling I had deep inside of me. My life was being presented before my mind's eye. All I could see was that I had lived thirty-one years for nothing, and no one.

"Before my conversion I had been a nominal Catholic. I rebelled against God because of the lack of a personal relationship and too much emotional pain. At the age of twelve, when this rebellion occurred, my father and mother separated, and I couldn't understand how God could let that happen. I ran from God and my family. I became involved with alcohol. Within a few years of drinking heavily, this habit led me into the use and abuse of other drugs: marijuana, hashish, LSD, MDA, amphetamines, barbiturates, and opiates: morphine, delaudid, and heroin. While I was involved with the drugs to the point of worship and addiction, I also entertained several different spiritual concepts. This position that life provided made me in great need of Jesus Christ's personal relationship.

"The way I had supported my drug addiction over the years had again put me behind bars. I had been busted with just a few pounds of marijuana—fourteen—and also charged with intent to distribute. Because I was carrying my gun, a stainless steel Smith & Wesson .38 Special, they also charged me with a concealed weapon. I knew from past experiences I could most likely avoid doing any major time, even though I was facing five to forty years in the Richmond State Prison.

"My thoughts were broken by the sound of someone walking towards my cell. I heard someone ask in a loud voice, 'Does anyone want a Bible or feel the need to pray?' Like a flash of lightning, I came off the bunk and clung to the cell bars. I heard myself say, 'I want a Bible. I need to pray.' It seemed like an instant when a large man appeared before me on the other side of the bars. He was holding a Bible like parents would hold their child in their arms. He had a warm look of concern and love in his face. He introduced himself as being Wayne Skinner, a minister from Outreach for Christ. As we shook hands, I introduced myself. He passed the Bible through the bars after our introductions, and it was opened to John 3:16. As I read it, tears came to my eyes. He suggested I read some other verses in the Gospel of John. When I was through reading, he asked me if I wanted to pray with him. I told him that I would, and as he prayed for Jesus to come into my heart, I really began to cry. As he prayed, I could feel something happening to me. The tears flowed heavily because God let me see my selfish sins. In my heart I told God I was sorry for my sins and wanted to live life differently than I had in the past. Then I knew because He lives, I would be able to change my life. Now I had a loving friend to help me. Wayne left me with an invitation to come and see him when I was let out of jail. That night I read all of John's Gospel and cried over every word. Sometimes I would cry with repentance, and at other times I cried with joy. The joyful tears came because I finally knew the Person of God. Writing of this experience fills me with God's Spirit to the point of chills and praise. Thank you, Jesus!

"The next day my lawyer had me released from jail. My old ways didn't attract me any longer, and I was driven by God's Spirit to find a local church to fellowship, study, and worship in. I was baptized and became a member of Oak Grove Baptist Church in Virginia Beach, Virginia."

Commentary on "Too Much Emotional Pain"

Chris was both a Lawbreaker and a Standard Flaunter. His lifestyle was certainly in conflict with traditional society. He bore the stigmas of prisoner, ex-convict, alcoholic, and drug addict. Congregations actively tend to exclude him and his kind, while at the same time he passively excluded them.

Can you think of any persons like Chris in your community? If so, does your congregation actively tend to exclude them? What specific outreach ministries do you have or support to reach your Chrises for Christ?

How did God get through to this thirty-one-year-old Locked-Out male? There was a God-shaped vacuum in Chris's life. From his earliest memory, he thought there was some kind of God. While sitting in jail, he had a cold and empty feeling deep down in his stomach. As he reviewed his life, he felt he had lived all of his years "for nothing, and no one." Our strategy for reaching Locked-Outs should probably pay some attention to that vacuum, either by assuming its presence or at least probing to see if it is there.

God sent Wayne Skinner to the right place at the right time to help the right man fill the emptiness and meaninglessness of his life. Clearly this was a "season of the soul" for Chris. He was ready and eager to hear God's messenger. We need to look for and seize these opportune times when persons are most receptive to the gospel. Paul was speaking about that in his instructions to the church at Colossae when he told them to make "the most of the time" (Col. 4:5).[3]

Skinner made his point of contact with the question: "Does anyone want a Bible or feel the need to pray?" What an excellent question for that context! Chris instantly came off his bunk and clung to the cell bars saying, "I want a Bible. I need to pray." Those who want a Bible and want to pray often want more and get more. Usually that is a sign of their receptivity to the gospel. Prayer may also be a sign of dependency upon some Higher Power.

This witness knew what he was doing by asking such a question. The messenger's point of contact was established at Chris's point of need. That was our Lord's method with Nicodemus (John 3:1-15), the woman of Samaria (John 4:4-42), the man who had been ill for thirty-eight years (John 5:2-18), and others. George G. Hunter, who heads the E. Stanley Jones School of Evangelism and World Mission at Asbury Theological Seminary in Wilmore, Kentucky, calls this kind of faith sharing inductive evangelism and offers two new inductive witnessing models built around Abraham Maslow's hierarchy of human motives.[4]

Skinner "had a warm look of concern and love in his face." Probably that warm look and love sharply contrasted with "the cold and empty feeling" in Chris. Our body language in witnessing either complements or contradicts or competes with our verbal language.

The gift Bible was open at John 3:16. Chris read that verse and some others in John's Gospel which Skinner suggested. Some call such verses from John's Gospel "the Johannine Road" in contrast with "the Roman Road" which uses selected verses primarily from the Book of Romans.

A prayer was offered by Skinner, with Chris's permission, for Jesus to come into Chris's heart. Chris did not make up his own prayer or repeat a suggested prayer offered by Skinner, either of which might have been done. Instead, "In my heart I told God I was sorry for my sins and wanted to live life differently than I had in the past," said he. Prayer at this crucial point in the gospel's presentation is vital, but there is no *one* way to draw the gospel net in prayer. Our rule should be to suit the prayer to the uniqueness and personal choice of each potential disciple.

The case does not tell us whether Skinner welcomed Chris into the family of God or shared a verse of assurance such as John 5:24. He did invite Chris to come and see him when he got out of jail. We recommend a new convert be immediately welcomed into the family of God through appropriate words and a handshake or better still a hug wherever that would be possible and appropriate.[5]

"A Completed Jew": The Case of Rachel Ben David[6]

Her maiden name was Rachel Ben David, the daughter of an orthodox Jewish rabbi. Rachel spent time in a Nazi concentration camp for no other reason than her race. She was married in Jerusalem at the age of fourteen to a man whom she had never seen and who had never seen her.

Rachel's husband, whom she called Joe, spoke English and Hebrew. She spoke only Hebrew. He was a big but gentle man standing six feet and ten inches tall while she was four feet and ten inches tall and weighed eighty pounds. They had a beautiful outdoor wedding in which they pledged to obey God instead of each other.

Rachel and Joe loved each other from that first day. They could not have children as they had hoped. Rachel was unable to bear children because of medical experiments conducted on her by the Nazis at Dachau. They left Palestine and settled down in Arizona.

Joe became a paratrooper and a Green Beret. While on a mission in Vietnam, he disappeared in 1968. First he was reported missing, then missing and presumed captured, and, finally, missing and presumed dead. Rachel never knew what happened. Joe went out and never came back.

Joe's death marked the end of one life for Rachel and the beginning of a new life which has brought her both joy and pain. The transition began with conversations between Rachel and a friend who was in an Old Testament course at Campbell University at Buies Creek, North Carolina. The two ladies discussed the Bible. One day Rachel decided to go to church with her friend just to see what went on there. "I was scared to death," said Rachel. "I had never been to a Christian church in my life."

Rachel liked what she saw and heard. She wanted to learn more. So she made an appointment with the pastor of the church. But the first thing she told the pastor was not to try to convert her.

That sensitive pastor gave Rachel a copy of the New Testament in Today's English Version. Rachel wouldn't even call it the Bible. Instead she called it "Mr. S's book," after the name of the pastor.

In April 1976, Rachel was on a plane to New York, and she was reading her New Testament. The place where she read was from the first chapter of Matthew, from what some call the "begats," which traces the genealogy of Jesus. "The more I read," said Rachel, "the more I knew these were my people; this was my family too. To me, it proved that Jesus was the Messiah the Jews had been promised."

Everything came together for Rachel at that moment. She discovered who Jesus was and who she was in relationship to Him. Rachel now lives a Christian life. She calls herself a "completed Jew."

The discovery of Jesus as her Messiah and Savior has brought deep joy to Rachel. She believes she is a better Jew because of her Christian faith and a better Christian because of her background in Judaism. The painful part of her new life is that her family has disowned her and held a funeral to mark her death.

Commentary on "A Completed Jew"

Rachel belonged to a different mold while living in Europe and the United States. She was a Jew living among Gentiles and, therefore, a member of an ethnic minority. The Nazis had put her in a concentration camp for no reason other than her race. She had never been in a Christian church in her life until she got to North Carolina.

The case helps us to see how strange we Christians appear to certain minorities among us. Rachel was not exaggerating when she said, "I was scared to death." We need to exert special effort to put at ease the Rachels among us.

That's one reason friendship evangelism is so crucial to the evangelization of ethnic minorities. Rachel's transition toward Christ began with conversations between her and a friend who was taking an Old Testament course. Genuine dialogue was taking place between them as they discussed the Bible. This was not a one-way monologue where the friend "dumped" her truck load of prepackaged gospel truths. Oh no! Rachel had something to give as well as to receive in this relationship. Christian witnesses are on both the giving and receiving ends when they share their faith.

It was natural for Rachel to go to church with her friend. Besides, Rachel was curious about what went on in those buildings Christians called churches. Such friendship and curiosity affords us a golden opportunity to say, "Come and see." That's what Philip said to Nathanael (John 1:46).

"People usually make contact with God in the same way we screw a lightbulb into an electrical socket . . . step by step and stage by stage" wrote Don Posterski.[7] Rachel's steps toward God in Christ are clearly traced in this case. The first step was her birth and upbringing in the home of an Orthodox Jewish rabbi where she was introduced to the one and only true God (see Rom. 9:4-5). The final step was when she became persuaded that Jesus was the Messiah while reading the "begats" of Matthew 1. We think there are as many as seven or eight additional steps. How many of those intervening steps can you identify, and what are they?

Several times Rachel started her life over: once when she was taken to Dachau; again when she went to live in Jerusalem; a third time when she married Joe whom she had never seen; a fourth time when she left Palestine for Arizona; a fifth time when Joe never came back from Vietnam; and, finally, when she became a "completed Jew." Change is not necessarily a catastrophe. It can be a turning point which leads to a fuller and more meaningful life. There is mounting evidence that persons undergoing transitions and major changes, such as those experienced by Rachel, are more receptive to the gospel and conversion.[8] That fact has weighty implications for an evangelism strategy intent on reaching dispersed persons.

Rachel called herself a "completed Jew." The 1980 Pattya miniconsultation on the evangelization of Jewish people concluded: "The Jew who is brought to faith in Christ does not cease being a Jew. Therefore, . . . he must be accorded the freedom in Christ to observe religious elements appropriate to him as an Israelite (e.g., Jewish religious festivals) so long as they are kept in a manner consistent with Scripture."[9]

In what ways does the gospel make a Jew "complete"? What do you think Rachel meant by concluding she is a better Jew because of her Christian faith and a better Christian because of her background in Judaism? What did it cost her to become a Christian?

"No One Seemed to Care": The Case of Jimbo[10]

In our community there lived a half-witted man named Jimbo. He and his mother lived together in an old shack at the end of a long, narrow drive. No one seemed to care about or for him and his aged mother.

Jimbo could be seen almost daily walking along the highway picking up trash and cans that had been thrown from vehicles by passing motorists. As far as I know, he had no personal friends. The children of the community were afraid of him even though he was a gentle soul. He lived a lonely, separated life. He was in the community, but he was definitely in no way a part of the community. Seemingly, because of his station in life, no one cared for his soul.

Almost a year after I had been saved, on a beautiful spring afternoon, a group of the youth of our church had been playing softball on a ball field adjacent to our church. I had been playing, but at this particular moment I was sitting on a bench resting. I looked up and saw Jimbo coming up the road. The power of the Holy Spirit impressed upon me that I should go to him and speak to him. I left the playground area and walked to where Jimbo was standing. Through new, God-given eyes I could see Jimbo as a precious creation of God and not as a half-wit. I was afraid. I had never talked to anyone about the need of Jesus as Savior. But I was also determined to tell Jimbo about Jesus. God gave me strength in my weakness and I gave my witness to this simple man. As I talked, he would say something. (I was never able to understand him completely when he would speak to me.) I continued to tell him how Christ had loosed me from my sin and that He wanted to do the same for him. When I completed my presentation of testimony, I invited Jimbo to accept Christ into his heart and to come be with us in church.

I felt somewhat defeated when Jimbo walked off because he would not make any definite commitment to the Lord. I had done what I thought was my best, but he seemed unconcerned.

But in a couple of weeks, Jimbo began to visit our church, and after several weeks he came forward during the time of invitation and publicly professed his acceptance of Christ as Savior. He was baptized and became a member of the church. His life was changed from one with no friends to one with many friends.

It is amazing how a person's worth changes in a community simply because one finds Christ and becomes a member of the local church. People, who seemingly would not take time to minister to Jimbo, now accepted him. We too often let our cultural and social bias blind our eyes to the needs of those not of our setting. When we allow this to happen in our lives, another determent to personal evangelism has overcome us.

Commentary on "No One Seemed to Care"

Jimbo had passively excluded the church; but in a couple of weeks after being invited, he began to attend. Only several weeks had passed when he owned Christ as his Lord and followed him in baptism and church membership. The case implies that Jimbo wanted friendship, acceptance, and new life.

The congregation was more attractive to Jimbo than he was to them. He wanted what the church had to offer more than the church wanted him and what he could offer. A church which salutes and seeks only her kind of people is like salt that never gets out of the saltshaker and into the world.[11] Her values fall far short of those of the upside-down kingdom of God (see Matt. 5:43-48).

Churches which actively exclude persons in their evangelizing exhibit a tendency to violate the foundational principle of dignity. The first and most basic principle of evangelism according to Christ was respect for human personality.[12] If we don't believe in the infinite worth and value of every human being, we will not so much as lift a little finger to evangelize those who are different or "strange" to us.

The case tells us that Jimbo was considered a half-witted man. He lived at the end of a long, narrow drive. No one seemed to care about him or his aged mother. His daily occupation was picking up trash and cans others had thrown out along the highway. He had no personal friends. The children were afraid of him as if he were some kind of ogre. "He was in the community, but . . . in no way a part of the community." Notice also the telling phrase, "his station in life." He was hard to understand when he spoke. The very name *Jimbo* sounds like a clown or an epithet and may devalue the man.

Does a person's worth change simply because he or she finds Christ and becomes a member of the church? The Bible teaches that every person is created in the image of God and is one for whom Christ died. Those of us who belong to the race of the twice-born are called and commissioned to see through "new, God-given eyes."

The first time anybody ever invited Jimbo to go to church, he went "in a couple of weeks." If we really want the Jimbos of our communities to come to Christ and to our churches, let's invite them and warmly welcome them when they come, as did the local church in this case. Something just that simple, if sincere, may work.

Notes

1. All of these cases, with the exception of a woman caught in adultery, are analyzed in separate chapters of Delos Miles, *How Jesus Won Persons,* (Nashville: Broadman Press, 1982), pp. 51-61, 123-130, 31-40, 131-140, 149-156, and 13-20, respectively.

2. This case was written by one of our students, Christopher A. Swalley, in July 1982 and is used with his permission.

3. For more on this principle of opportunism, see Delos Miles, *Master Principles of Evangelism* (Nashville: Broadman Press, 1982), pp. 40-46.

4. George G. Hunter, III, *The Contagious Congregation,* pp. 38-59.

5. For detailed suggestions and bibliography on follow-up and conservation, see Delos Miles, "Follow-Up and Conservation," *Introduction to Evangelism,* (Nashville: Broadman Press, 1983), pp. 355-366.

6. The facts in this case are based on Dennis Rogers, "Life of Abrupt Changes Brings Intense Pain, Deep Joy," *The News and Observer,* 23 June 1983, p. 1C, Raleigh, N.C.

7. Don Posterski, *Why Am I Afraid to Tell You I'm a Christian?* (Downers Grove, Ill.: Inter-Varsity Press, 1983), p. 54.

8. For some of that evidence, see Delos Miles, *Church Growth—A Mighty River* (Nashville: Broadman Press, 1981), pp. 90-94.

9. *Lausanne Occasional Papers No. 7, Thailand Report - Christian Witness to the Jewish People,* Lausanne Committee for World Evangelization, p. 17.

10. This case was written by one of our students, John Lawrence, in April 1984 and is used with his permission.

11. See Rebecca Manley Pippert, *Out of the SaltShaker & into the World* (Downers Grove, Ill.: Inter-Varsity Press, 1979).

12. On the principle of dignity in evangelization, see Delos Miles, *Master Principles of Evangelism,* pp. 11-19. 11-19.

8
The Opt-Outs: Not My People

Opt-Outs are hard-to-reach persons who have taken a stance against the church as they perceive it and, perhaps, against faith. Some have examined religion and have chosen to be actively anti-church like the philosophic atheists. Others have selected a secular or hedonistic approach to life; for them the church is insignificant and impractical. Both groups intend to live outside the church. This intentional choice is often experienced as threatening by local congregations who then exclude the Opt-Outs from their active outreach efforts.

Opt-Outs have decided they can live without the church. The rich young ruler (Matt. 19:16-22) made his faith choice and became an Opt-Out. Augustine, C. S. Lewis, and Malcolm Muggeridge were Opt-Outs too during their pre-Christian days.[1] For the most part, Opt-Outs have excluded themselves from church involvement by their personal choices.

Out by Choice

Who falls in the Opt-Out category? A variety of hard-to-reach folk live outside of institutional religion by choice.
- Philosophical atheists who don't believe in God
- Political groups who exclude religion or who make politics their religion
- Persons who substitute volunteer organizations or fraternal orders for the church
- Hedonists and pleasure seekers

- Secularists who live as if God makes no practical difference in life
- Nomads whose jobs or life-styles hinder them from putting down organizational roots, including church ties
- Religious cults
- Persons who are adherents of other world religions
- Modern-day "publicans" who view church members as hypocrites
- Persons who are devoted to hobbies or leisure activities

Not every Opt-Out has engaged in a long, detached, rational decision-making process. But the result of their choice is the same. Opt-Outs don't plan to give local congregations any time or space in their daily lives. That stance makes them hard-to-reach.

Grouping the Opt-Outs

The Opt-Out category subdivides into three groups: the Philosophical Unbelievers, the Replacement Religions, and the Seekers After Truth. Each group has selected a way of life outside the institutional church.

The Philosophical Unbelievers

This group is made up of persons who are outspoken in their opposition to the personal practice of religious faith.

The village atheists. Hale found few classical atheists in his interviews with America's unchurched. Hale suspects many unbelievers don't want to accept the stigma a public stance of unbelief would bring. Therefore, few Americans openly describe themselves as irreligious.[2] Martin Marty claims atheists' conventions could be held in a phone booth.

Atheism in contemporary America may be more akin to one of the term's original meanings. The Romans called the early Christians atheists because they denied more gods than they accepted. According to the Roman viewpoint, the more gods one worshiped, the more "religious" one was. Many Americans, like the Romans, accept lots of deities. Contemporary idolatry makes the agnostic or old-fashioned atheist fairly rare in America today.

Worldwide, however, atheists are more numerous. One hundred and ninety-seven million people, or about four percent of the world's population, consciously call themselves atheists. Atheism is the official governmental stance in thirty countries. Atheists' numbers are increasing by roughly 8.5 million persons yearly.[3] These persons are obviously hard to reach with the Christian message.

The secularists. More numerous in America are folk who live as if God doesn't make an impact on daily living. Secularists aren't necessarily antichurch; they simply ignore matters of faith in life. The secular mind-set excludes religious values. One secularist told Hale, "I don't know what people are talking about when they say 'God' or 'religion,' . . . I just don't think religious thoughts, don't know when I last did . . . I have my problems—everybody has them—but neither the churches nor religion can help me. I've got to do my best with my noodle up here."[4] Opting out of the church are those in the secularist camp. These hard-to-reach persons aren't apt to cut down the distance between themselves and churches. They feel no need or interest. We'll have to approach them with the gospel.

Replacement religions

Many Americans fill the God-shaped void in their lives with other than God. Sports, volunteer activities, the pursuit of pleasure, and politics are prime candidates for substitute faiths.

The sports enthusiasts. Recently an elderly widow told me, "Every Saturday of our marriage my husband went hunting or fishing. I wish I'd had the nerve just once to say, 'Mr. Smith, this is your day at home with your children. *I'm* going out today.' " My friend was married to the kind of person who chooses leisure pursuits over family and church.

For some Americans, the stadium has replaced the cathedral,

other fans the congregation, and the sports page the Bible. Since moving to the South, I've become curious about the NASCAR auto-racing circuit. I've noticed some folk are fanatical about "goin' racin.' " For example, when the World 600 was run at the Charlotte Motor Speedway in 1981, over 100 thousand fans attended and spent an estimated 32 million dollars. It sounds like sports get the tithe too.

Edna and Martha are racing fans without peer. They follow the thirty-one Grand National races with their husbands. They dish out sandwiches and sympathy to the drivers and crews. Edna and Martha provide food for the drivers. They spend seventy to one hundred dollars of their own money at the grocery every day they're at the track just to feed the drivers. Sound like a religion? Here's how they are characterized: "Unique ladies, Edna Hollon and her friend, Martha Kemp. They're missionaries of a sort, angels of mercy who are in love with stock car racing and the men who gamble it all for the thrill and rewards of a ride to victory circle."[5] Folk who invest at least thirty-one weekends a year in sports are apt to be Opt-Outs and become hard-to-reach.

The volunteer helpers. For some people, Scouts, lodges, 4-H, Rotary, Weight Watchers, or the volunteer fire department replace religion. One of my students did an organizational study of our local rescue squad. Why had men voluntarily joined an emergency services unit? To conquer their fear of death. That's a religious issue fundamentally. Were there any Baptists on our rescue squad? No. Somehow the Baptist churches and our rescue squad were apparently operating on separate but parallel tracks. Volunteer organizations can become substitutes for religion.

The allegiance pledgers. Other Opt-Outs invest themselves in political activity. They involve themselves in social issues or partisan causes for nonreligious reasons. They demonstrate that no person can serve two masters.

The Seekers After Truth

Some Opt-Outs aren't necessarily faithless; they don't place their energies in Christian churches though. Obvious in this group are persons who belong to religious cults or other world religions. Other Opt-Outs see hypocrisy in churches or simply choose to live their religion outside of traditional congregations.

The publicans. Like the contrasting of Pharisees and publicans in Luke 18, these folk view church members as hypocrites who live by a double standard. According to Hale, "Hardly any of my informants fall outside this category. The charge that church people are hypocrites, phonies, fakers was made, at least in passing, by almost all of those with whom I spoke."[6]

The churchless believers. Some believers don't believe in the church. As one who felt a Christian life could be lived outside the church told Hale, "I think the churches have gotten like a lot of parts of society. They have to worry so much about paying the rent that they have forgotten the good news. They forget the evangelized message. They forget love."[7] Disillusionment with the institution doesn't necessarily mean faithlessness to the churchless believers. But they opt out of local congregations.

Why do over sixty million Americans say they are believers but choose not to belong to any congregation? Why do they say yes to faith but no to churches? Why do they divorce believing from belonging?

Most of these churchless believers apparently see religion as strictly a private matter. They see no reason to link with any religious community. Other churchless believers feel churches are more organized than spiritual. Surprisingly, most of these folk have grown up in traditional religious backgrounds.

There's some good news about the churchless believers though. A majority of them can envision circumstances in which they would join a worshiping and ministering fellowship. We should stay close to these hard-to-reach types so we can seize the moment of readiness and invite them into active church life.[8]

Faith Demonstration as a Strategy

Opt-Outs need to reexamine authentic Christian living "up close and personal." Rather than declaring them the "prospects," we may need to see ourselves as the prospects and demonstrate for them the practical impacts of Christianity. For example, the early Christian martyrs were said to have "out lived and out died" their persecutors. If Stephen had not died in the manner he did, Paul might never have preached as he did. The modern parallel may be that we will have to "out live" competing philosophies by demonstrating the peace and joy of Christian faith.

Specifically, what do the Opt-Outs need relationally and theologically? The Philosophic Unbelievers are excluded by their overt antagonism to the church. They need Christian friends who are willing to live with the tension of disagreeing agreeably about religious issues. Keeping the conversation open and amiable may allow further revelation to break through.

Followers of Replacement Religions are out of the church because they've substituted one faith for another. They need to know Christians who express a concern for both faith and special interests. For instance, I befriended a golfing devotee whose health only allowed him to play in the cool of the early mornings. After several prebreakfast rounds of golf, he said, "I've never had a friend who was a preacher before." I'd never teed off before my bacon and eggs either, but the effort was worth it to me for the sake of this Opt-Out friend.

Seekers After Truth have made a prior commitment to themselves or to another religious perspective. They need a Christian model, a comparative life to measure themselves against. Fundamentally, this approach incarnates Christ for others just as He incarnated God for us.

Walking in another person's shoes and seeing life from that

perspective may be a new and risky experience for some of us. But our risks may allow Opt-Outs to make a new decision for Christian faith.

Options for Reaching the Opt-Out

Reaching Opt-Outs requires patience and persistence. Although evangelizing Opt-Outs is slow work, several strategies show promise.

Dialogue

Since the Opt-Out has taken an antichurch position, listening to his reasons for excluding himself from the church is a beginning point for ministry. Discovering his perception of the church or his experience with particular congregations opens the door for conversation about the nature of the Christian life and the church. Because Opt-Outs have closed themselves out of the church, dialogue offers the possibility of cultivating a new consideration of the Christian faith as a life-style.

Practice

Being patiently available to people allows you to be present at the teachable moments in their lives. Whether the occasion is a tragic event or the awakening of a life because of the Holy Spirit's ripening work, let's be present when faith's knock of opportunity occurs for Opt-Outs.

Consistency

Many Opt-Outs are alert to any inconsistency in Christians' lives which they can use to support their misconceptions of religion. Consistency in belief and behavior, therefore, is crucial in reaching persons who have chosen to stay out of the church. We may be faced with returning seventy times seven times before Opt-Outs respond to the gospel in faith.

Forays into Hostile Territories

Opt-Outs can show open hostility toward Christians. Witness
to them becomes a painful process when hostility is expressed
toward us. Many of us are probably too thin skinned when we
encounter slammed doors, cutting put-down remarks, or crafty
debaters. In the face of hostility, we tend to become either defen-
sive or combative. I became cooler under fire when I decided God
was big enough to take care of Himself and his gospel. I don't play
as many games since I no longer feel a need to defend God. My
responsibility is to share as winsomely and persuasively as possible what He has done and is doing in my life. Witnessing without returning hostility will make forays into the hostile territories
of the Opt-Outs an exchange, not a battle.

Notes

1. The cases of these three are found in Hugh T. Kerr and John T.
Molder, eds., *Conversions: the Christian Experience* (Grand Rapids: Wm. B.
Eerdmans Publishing Co., 1983), pp. 11-14, 199-204, and 251-254.

2. J. Russell Hale, *The Unchurched* (San Francisco: Harper and Row, 1980),
p. 160.

3. "Number of Atheists Reported Increasing," *Baptist Messenger*, 1 Mar.
1984, p. 4.

4. Ibid., p. 163.

5. Gerald Martin, "For Edna and Martha, Racing No Casual Affair,"
News and Observer, 24 May 1981, p. 5-II.

6. Hale, p. 156.

7. Ibid., p. 113.

8. "The Unchurched American," *Grapevine*, Jan. 1984, pp. 1-3.

9
Case Studies of Evangelized Opt-Outs

Both in the previous chapter and in this one, we lift up the rich young ruler (Mark 10:17-22) as a biblical case of an Opt-Out whom Jesus sought to win to Himself. An official whose son was ill (John 4:46-54) may be another opt-out case in the Gospels.[1] The three contemporary cases which follow illustrate some of the strategies for reaching Opt-Outs discussed in chapter 8.

"Decided to Go to Hell": The Case of Bob Dale

My childhood is full of church memories. I remember outdoor revival meetings. I remember my dad's profession of faith during his late twenties. Most of all, I remember spending mornings in the Sunday School at Cave Springs Baptist Church near Neosho, Missouri.

I remember going to Sunday School as a preschooler. Our classroom was a curtained area on the right side of the pulpit platform. We sat around a low table and heard the great stories of the Bible told, saw colored pictures of biblical scenes, and watched flannelgraph presentations. One of my most vivid memories of childhood in church is giving my offering—my mother always tied up some coins in the corner of my handkerchief, and I usually had a struggle getting my small fingers to master the knots.

An awakening occurred in my life during a morning worship service when I was eight or nine years old. I have no idea who the preacher was or what he had said. But I remember exactly how I felt. I even remember where my mother and

I were seated that day—near the front on the left side of the building. At the end of the service, the pastor gave an invitation for any person who wanted to make a Christian commitment. Suddenly, I felt like someone had inflated a balloon inside me. I thought I might explode. I had no way of recognizing that the Holy Spirit was convicting me and ripening me for salvation. I only knew I was uncomfortable. In order to distract myself, I peered out of the window and watched a crew of threshers working in a nearby field. This feeling of internal pressure stayed with me. Every time I came to church—especially during the invitation hymns—and whenever my family listened to "The Greatest Story Ever Told" radio program, I felt over-inflated. Gradually I realized that the Holy Spirit was dealing with me, and I knew clearly that I needed to become a Christian.

The next spring during my fourth grade school year, Cave Springs held one of its two annual revival meetings. By now I had "graduated" from sitting with my parents during church services and sat at the rear of the sanctuary with my friends of the same age. Revivals were always well attended since church provided one of the community's key social events. Like most of our revivals, this revival focused on Christians early in the week and then zeroed in on the lost as the week wore on.

On Wednesday evening, I was seated on the back row with my friend, Webbie (short for Webster). The invitation was extended through numerous stanzas, and each additional verse of singing seemed like an eternity because the Holy Spirit was dealing with me intensively. Out of the corner of my eye I saw Webbie edging out into the aise. He stood in the aisle for a moment and then stepped back between the pews and stayed beside me until the service was over. The next day at school Webbie and I were together on the playground during recess. Webbie asked, "Did you see what I did last night during the invitation?" "No," I lied while I felt that sense of inner pressure building up again. "I almost went forward and gave my life to Christ," Webbie said. "And tonight I'm going to become a Christian!" I didn't respond to Webbie's statement, but I made myself a promise. "Tonight I'm going to sit by Webbie again," I told myself, "When Webbie goes forward, I will too. Tonight I'm going to become a Christian!"

I went home after school with lots of expectations. But a surprise was in store for me. I did my farm chores and homework, ate supper, and got ready for church. My parents misinterpreted my quietness. My mother announced, "You've been to the revival every night and seem tired. Since tomorrow's a school day, you and I will stay at home so you can get to bed early. Daddy and your brother will go on to church tonight by themselves." I pleaded and cried but had to stay at home anyway. I couldn't find the courage to tell my parents that I wanted to become a Christian that night. Later in my bed I made a decision. Feeling my hurt and disappointment keenly, I reasoned that my parents wouldn't let me go to church. They must not want me to become a Christian. They must want me to go to hell. After considering that sobering possibility, I decided that was exactly what I'd do. I'd "show" them. I'd never become a Christian. I'd go to hell on purpose.

It was a stupid, childish choice. But I lived out that decision for almost a decade. It wasn't easy. I was in church every time the doors were open. I tithed every penny I made. I read my Bible every day. I was a moral person and chose my circle of friends from other kids who were churchgoers. I learned more Bible than any of the other kids. In fact, I taught the Adult Men's Sunday School class every year during Youth Week. My parents, friends, pastors, and every evangelist who came to my church talked with me about becoming a

Christian. But I stubbornly stuck by my guns. I might be a good person, but I'd never become a Christian. I had opted out of Christianity.

The inner turmoil of my teen years was almost beyond description. I had all of the usual teenager's questions and self-doubts. But overlaying these normal problems was the deep unrest growing out of my confirmed resistance to God. I knew that I needed Christ. I knew how to become a Christian. Instead of accepting Christ as my Savior, I lived with fear, guilt, and risk.

Late in my high school career, my father had a new well drilled to provide water for our family. As the well was being finished, it began to bubble. The well driller struck a match to examine the problem and discovered (when the well caught fire) that he had brought in a gas well. Dad and the driller capped the well and lighted the release valve. The gas light gave a soft, eerie quality to the night's darkness around our home. One Sunday evening, I was at home alone recovering from an illness when my mother returned from church after Training Union in order to have an hour to talk with me again about becoming a Christian. She sat on the end of my bed and told me once again how much she wished I'd give my life to Christ. I recall that she hadn't switched on the lamp in my room, and as night fell the shadows of the gas light played across the ceiling. When my mother left the room, I prayed for forgiveness. I immediately felt peaceful for the first time since that "balloon" had been blown up! I imaged a pond without a ripple of movement on it. The sense of tranquillity was a welcome guarantee that I'd just made a significant, correct decision.

My pattern of resistance continued however. I'd said no to God so consistently for so long that I'd turned it into a dangerous game. Even though I'd become a Christian, I didn't tell anyone. Several months later during another revival I talked with my pastor and the visiting evangelist. They helped me see that I'd already made my commitment and only needed to declare my faith publicly. I did and was baptized the week before I went away to college.

The next sixteen months almost gave me the spiritual "bends." In one fell swoop, I went from being the community agnostic to the resident Christian on my floor of one of the University of Missouri's dormitories. I joined a college church several miles away from my dormitory. An upperclassman who accepted my invitation to go to church thought the walk was too long and complained, "You don't go to church on Sunday. You go on a pilgrimage!" On another occasion, I was a little stunned when two students burst into my room and one demanded of the other, "Now you ask Bob. He'll tell you there's a God!" After this impromptu theological lecture, I asked why I'd been chosen to settle their dispute. Their answer? Because I had a Bible on my dresser. At the end of my freshman year in college, I felt called to preach and committed my life to the ministry. In only six more weeks, a tiny Baptist church in the Missouri mountains asked me to be their pastor. In just a few brief months, I moved from an opt-out stance toward Christ to serving as a pastor. The change was rapid and radical. But I much preferred the concerns of caring for others in Christ's name to the uneasiness of trying deliberately to go to hell.

Commentary on "Decided to Go to Hell"

Not all Opt-Outs are adults—at least not when they initially decide to make their stance against faith. Bob was less than ten years old when he made up his mind never to become a Christian and to intentionally go to hell. We may agree with him that it was "a stupid, childish choice." Nevertheless, he lived out that decision about a decade. One implication of this for congregational strategy in reaching Opt-Outs is the need to acknowledge that some children can make very weighty decisions.

Let us ponder long and deep what Bob said about the awakening in his life during a morning worship service when he was eight or nine years old: "I had no way of recognizing that the Holy Spirit was convicting me and ripening me for salvation." He was under conviction and didn't know it. Nor did he right then know what to do. This "season of the soul," when he was especially receptive to salvation, continued for some months until the incident with Webbie and his parents' decision to keep him out of the revival services that momentous Thursday night of his early life.

Gospel receptivity mysteriously ebbs and flows. Christian parents and all who would evangelize should pray for sensitivity to the Spirit's leadership in the lives of their Bobs.[2]

We may be reluctant to admit it, but some Opt-Outs have been reared in Christian homes and churches. Bob tells us that his childhood was full of church memories. Especially did he remember revival meetings, Sunday School, worship services, and public invitations. Even after Bob's decision to opt out of becoming a Christian, he steadfastly continued to be what he called a "moral" and "good" person. That meant he was in church every time the doors were open; tithed every penny he made; read his Bible every day; chose his circle of friends from among other church kids; learned more Bible "than any of the other kids"; and taught the Adult Men's Sunday School Bible class every year during Youth Week.

Many Opt-Outs see themselves as good and moral persons. They are the rich young rulers of our communities. Can we affirm their wholesome and commendable features as did Jesus (Luke 18:18-30) but then go on to teach them, "No one is good but God alone," and "One thing you still lack"? Furthermore, if they turn away sorrowfully because our gospel is too costly, do we continue to love them as did He? (Compare Matt. 19:16-22; Mark 10:17-22; Luke 18:18-30.)

A commendable feature in this case is the loving persistence with which Bob's parents, friends, pastors, and visiting evangelists pursued him and sought to persuade him to become a Christian. They never let go of him in spite of his stubborn resistance. We may be tempted to give up on Opt-Outs too quickly.

"The Resident Atheist": The Case of Old John[3]

"How do you preachers know there is a God?" he said, sitting on the edge of his wife's bed in the hospital room. She was shocked at his remark and obviously uncomfortable, probably the main reason he said it. Behind me I could hear Coy Ball gasping for breath. He had met old John before and didn't want to get into a conversation with him now if he could help it.

"What do you mean?" I replied in my calmest twenty-three-year-old preacher voice. "You folk don't know all that stuff you're always talking about," he went on. "Where is heaven? Up?" He laughed, knowing he had me now. "Why we've sent rockets up there and proved there wasn't no heaven upstairs." He gave a long, satisfied look, waiting to see what I would say.

"Guess I can't argue with that," I said, "they didn't see anything up there." "You know how big heaven is?" he went on. I didn't. "I thought you preachers knew your Bible. Book of Revelation says it's fifteen hundred miles on a side (Rev. 21:16)—that ain't big as the United States. How you going to fit all the Chinese and Mexicans and dead people in a little ole place like that? If half the people go to heaven who say they will, it'll be standing room only. You don't expect me to believe that, now do you?"

The fact of the matter was that for all his bantering skepticism John was very serious about God. He was right; we didn't have all the answers. We didn't have all the right questions. Only when I admitted that did old John know that I took God as seriously as he did.

Some months after I first met him, old John was found to have tuberculosis. His wife had gotten well and left the hospital, but John got steadily worse over the next year, and, finally, he died from the disease. When the tuberculosis was first diagnosed, most church folk seemed to think that it was the judgment of God. After all, John had for years been the resident atheist and blasphemed all the local church doctrines with which he was familiar. When I saw John in the hospital and asked him what *he* thought it was, characteristically he responded, "Well, I think it is tuberculosis!"

In my own way, I tried to act out the Christmas story for John. I visited him without fail in the hospital; he never went home. More than anything else, I think, this impressed him, for most everyone else was scared of the tuberculosis or the atheism, so they didn't come to see him. At every visit, we talked about God and what He might think about the rough life John had lived. I spoke of grace and the Cross. After months, John allowed me to read to him from the Bible. From that day on, I read it at every visit and until he died.

Some people won't accept this, but there is a lot of evangelism about which we can never be certain. A person's acceptance or rejection of God is not always black or white to us. John never spoke familiar words like we teach people to say when they accept Christ. But I believe that John trusted Christ and that I will see my old friend on Resurrection Day.

Commentary on "The Resident Atheist"

Old John threatened some Christians with his bantering skepticism. His opening remark in the case shocked his sick wife and made her visibly uncomfortable. It left Coy Ball gasping for breath. Coy had no desire to get into a conversation with old John.

Nor do most of us Christians. Our tendency is to make social pariahs out of the old Johns in our midst.

When old John got tuberculosis, most church folk seemed to think it was the judgment of God. They were scared of the disease or the atheism or both and didn't go to see him. For the most part, they let his physical problem isolate them even farther from their resident atheist and blasphemer.

The big problem with such a strategy of separation and isolation is: How do we lead persons to Christ if we have no contact with them? Perhaps one reason we don't lead more old Johns to Christ is that we don't want to have anything to do with them. Jonah wasn't the only witness who sought to flee his mission.

Was old John really an atheist? Pastor Barnett said, "John was very serious about God." Only when the young pastor admitted that he didn't have all the answers, or even all the right questions, was some rapport established between them.

The first service Pastor Barnett rendered old John was to listen to him. Christian witnesses should strive to become expert listeners. Dietrich Bonhoeffer in *Life Together* told us the first ministry we Christians owe another person is to listen to him or her.

Beyond that elementary and basic service of lending a listening ear, the twenty-three-year-old pastor tried to act out the Christmas story. He sought to flesh out the gospel so old John could see it, smell it, touch it, taste it, and hear it. He visited John without fail in the hospital from which he never went home. On every visit, they talked about God while the pastor spoke of grace and the Cross. We can imagine that joyful day, after months of trying to faithfully live out the good news, when old John allowed his new friend to read the Bible to him. If you had been in the pastor's place, which Scriptures would you have read to old John on those succeeding visits?

Church growth theoreticians and practictioners like to talk about the three *Ps* in evangelism: presence, proclamation, and persuasion. *Presence evangelism* is being the good news; it is being with and ministering to persons in the name of Christ. *Proclamation evangelism* is proclaiming Jesus Christ as Lord and Savior; it is presenting the claims of Christ in the lives of persons and making a call for commitment. *Persuasion evangelism* seeks to lead persons into a life-changing relationship with Jesus Christ and responsible church membership; it tries to persuade persons to become Christ's disciples and responsible members of His church.[4]

Based on your understanding of these three types of evangelism and the case, which type(s) of evangelism did Pastor Barnett practice with old John? Which type(s) of the three *Ps* are you following in trying to evangelize the old Johns of your Jerusalem?

"What's God Got for Me?": The Case of Jim Johnson

My witnessing experience with a young soldier named Jim Johnson is memorable because of the unusual way it began and because of the vigor with which Jim is now serving Christ. Home on furlough, Jim decided to visit our church in south Saint Joseph. He had been in a great deal of trouble in the army, was not getting along with either of his parents, had been involved in the Church of Satan, had read their sacred book, and was totally alienated from God, others, and himself. The note Jim wrote at the bottom of his visitor's card that Sunday night summed up his inner longings: "What's God got for me?"

One of the deacons, Leroy, who was himself a personal witness, saw the card that night and let me know he wanted to go with me on that follow-up visit. When I called Jim to make an appointment, he was very cordial but told me not to come to the door because his dad hated preachers. So, on Tuesday night, Leroy and I picked Jim up at the end of the lane and went to a truck stop for a cup of coffee. Jim told it all: his dissatisfaction with his life, his searching for meaning through drugs, the Church of Satan, his inner scars from broken family relationships, and much more.

Over many cups of coffee, Leroy and I listened, seemingly taking turns interjecting comments now and then or asking questions for clarification. Finally, it was as if Jim stopped his story to hear what we could offer him. At first, the usual points in the plan of salvation were presented; and the usual arguments were offered in return: too much suffering in the world to believe in God, too many hypocrites, and on and on.

Somehow that night, Leroy and I both sensed God's presence in an unusual way. Everything "clicked." Though we could not talk to each other about it at that time, we have often talked of it since, and we remember both thinking that this was no routine follow-up visit. We both avoided any head-on argument with Jim about the issues he was raising. Instead, we talked with him about God's marvelous love and what it had meant to us. I am sure Jim thought that Leroy and I had planned our strategy beforehand, but it was truly an impression we both sensed from God's Spirit. Jim's resistance began to melt, his countenance changed subtly, and he warmed up. I believe Jim felt frustrated because we would not argue with him and also because we refused to pressure him. Over and over, from every conceivable angle, we talked of a loving, personal Savior.

We took Jim home and left him in a very thoughtful and bewildered state. The following Sunday night as I was making final preparation for my evening message, Jim appeared in my office doorway. He told me exactly what he wanted to do. He wanted to be saved, and right then! I showed him a few Scriptures, then he prayed for the Lord to save him. He wept on bended knees and simply poured his heart out to God. At the close of that evening's service, Jim made his public decision.

He shipped out to Korea soon after that, and his letters

told me of continued growth in Christ and his comradeship with a helpful chaplain. Our church kept praying for Jim and considered him our missionary in Korea. He has now married and visits us whenever time permits. Every time I see the joy of the Lord in Jim's eyes, I know I am seeing an answer to Jim's own question: "What's God got for me?"

Commentary on "What's God Got for Me?"

Jim was one of those Opt-Outs who was a seeker after truth. Perhaps he had been influenced to choose against Christianity by his father who hated preachers. His search for truth had taken him into the Church of Satan and led him to read their sacred book. It even brought him to visit a church in Saint Joseph, Missouri. Pastor Sager and Leroy, a deacon, were able to capitalize on that search for truth in Jim's pilgrimage.

Coupled with Jim's search for truth was alienation, dissatisfaction, and rebellion. He was alienated from God, others, and himself; he wasn't getting along with his parents; he had been in a great deal of trouble in the Army, and he had sought meaning through drugs. That accounts in some measure for the sarcastic note he wrote on his visitor's card, "What's God got for me?"

The case assumes a follow-up visit would be made to Jim. The best prospects a church has are those who take the initiative in visiting the congregation. Moreover, the quicker we follow up on our visitors, the better are our chances for reaching them. Jim worshiped with this church on Sunday night. The pastor and deacon visited him on Tuesday night, and he made his profession of faith the following Sunday night. Because Opt-Outs like Jim Johnson so seldom take the initiative in visiting churches, we believe an immediate follow-up visit to them may be needed.

Doyle and Leroy first listened to Jim's story. They heard him out, occasionally taking turns interjecting appropriate comments and asking questions. Jim's question on the visitor's card may have forewarned them that he had something which he wanted to get "off his chest." Sensitive listening is always important but especially so in witnessing to hard-to-reach persons.

After the witnessing team had patiently heard Jim's story, he seemed ready to hear their story. They did not argue with Jim but, sensing God's presence in an unusual way, told him the old, old story of God's marvelous love as they had experienced it in their own lives. They followed Ralph Sockman's advice that an ounce of honest testimony is worth a whole ton of argument.

The case reveals a strong sense of dependency upon the Holy Spirit in the witnesses. They "sensed God's presence in an unusual way." Their witnessing strategy that Tuesday night "was truly an impression we both sensed from God's Spirit." Jim's resistance began to melt, and he warmed up to them and their message because of the Spirit's work. Evangelizing is spiritual work done by spiritual persons endued with the power of God's Spirit.[6]

How well do you think those two witnesses answered Jim's question: "What's God got for me?" What is your congregation doing to answer similar questions put to you by the Jim Johnsons in your sphere of influence?

Notes

1. These two cases are analyzed in Delos Miles, *How Jesus Won Persons* (Nashville: Broadman Press, 1982), pp. 103-112, and 63-74.

2. For specific suggestions and bibliography on evangelizing children, see Delos Miles, "Evangelizing Children," *Introduction to Evangelism* (Nashville: Broadman Press, 1983) pp. 321-332.

3. This case is from a sermon by Dr. Marion C. Barnett, preached at Temple Baptist Church, Champaign, Illinois, December 25, 1983, and is used with his permission.

4. For a fuller and somewhat different discussion of the three *P*s in evangelism, see C. Peter Wagner, *Church Growth and the Whole Gospel* (San Francisco: Harper & Row, Publishers, 1981), pp. 55-57.

5. This case was written by one of our students, Rev. Doyle Sager, several years ago, and is used with his permission.

6. For a much fuller treatment of the principle of dependency in evangelism, see Delos Miles, "Dependency," *Master Principles of Evangelism*, (Nashville: Broadman Press, 1982), pp. 59-69.

10
Tailoring Evangelism for the Hard-to-Reach

Discussion about churchless Americans has turned a corner recently. The studies of the unchurched during the 1970s focused mostly on who the churchless are and what they think. But the 1980s appear to be cultivating a discussion on how to reach the unchurched for Christ. We're switching from a focus on the "outs" to how to get them "in" the church. Schools of thought have grown up around the old and new ways of looking at the unchurched.

But What Do I Do?

The "out school" has led the exploration of the unchurched previously. Gallup and the demographers identified the "typical" churchless American. The pollsters' findings were often interesting, sometimes frightening. We were left a bit frustrated by their analyses however. Since statistically the typical unchurched American is a blue-collar Oregonian, should we all become lumberjacks in the Cascade Mountains in order to make our evangelistic contributions? What do Gallup's statistics mean for us?

Then Russell Hale advanced the state of the art for the "out school." Hale spent a year interviewing churchless Americans in six highly unchurched counties from Maine, West Virginia, Florida, and Alabama to California and Oregon. Hale's contributions include hearing and recording unchurched persons' atrocity stories and categorizing and naming the unchurched by terms like the Boxed-In, the Burned-Out, and the Floaters. Hale moved beyond impersonal statistics to face-to-face contact and learning about the unchurched from the unchurched themselves. There's a fire and feeling about his book *The Unchurched* that's fresh and new in the studies of churchless Americans. Still, two problems persisted in our psyches. First, Hale tells us "who" without much "how to." He describes the unchurched person beautifully but doesn't deal much with how to reach our churchless neighbors. We're still left wondering what to do now. Second, we recognize Hale's prospect list came from local ministers. Did they have eyes to see all the hard-to-reach Left-Outs, Drop-Outs, Locked-Outs, and Opt-Outs? Was Hale's sample typical of most of our neighborhoods?

The "out school" method of studying the unchurched left some of us somewhat frustrated and pessimistic. They identified an overwhelming host of nonchurched people in our country. They discovered that many of the unchurched are at best suspicious and at worst hostile at us in the church. Their reports are almost enough to make us want to circle the wagons and call in the cavalry! Personally, we probably can deal with our frustration at the size and difficulty of the task. What bothers us most is the sense of pessimism we get after we read and hear the "out school" viewpoint. Where the gospel's good news is concerned, we don't intend to remain pessimistic.

Foundations to Build On

That's why we like the tone of the newer "in school" of discussion about churchless Americans. The "in school" has taken the "out school" information and started using it to build evangelism and ministry strategies.

Edward Rauff's *Why People Join the Church* and Carl Dudley's *Where Have All Our People Gone?* are good illustrations of the "in school's" more practical bent. For instance, Rauff wondered why Gallup's polls found so many persons who considered themselves believers but who were unchurched. Intrigued by Hale's interviews, Rauff decided to visit the same six counties as Hale (plus an additional county in Michigan) and ask people about their "back-to-church

pilgrimage." He interviewed 180 persons. Two were persons con-
tacted by Hale two years earlier, Both of these persons had joined
churches in the two-year interim between Hale and Rauff's studies. Rauff agrees with Roozen's discovery that many Drop-Outs
are really "phase outs." Roozen found that 46 percent of Americans drop out of active religious participation for at least two years
sometime during their lifetime. Then 80 percent return. Phase out,
phase in.[1]

How to Reach Unchurched Americans

Why do the unchurched join congregations? Rauff found several recurring themes in his interviews.[2] Notice the diversity of
reasons. Apparently, we must become all things to everybody
rather than look for the one and only, correct way to reach the
unchurched. Christians need a variety of strategies—informal as
well as formal—for evangelizing the hard-to-reach.

Influence of Christian People

About one in eight of the unchurched saw a difference in the
quality of life in a friend, relative, or co-worker and connected the
difference to faith or church affiliation. Love and spontaneous
witness made more impact on these interviewees than planned
evangelism.

Family Relationships and Responsibilities

The dominant reason respondents older than thirty gave for
returning to church was strengthening family life. Robert Gribbon, in a study for the Alban Institute, predicts the baby boom
generation now in its thirties will begin returning to the church
during the 1980s. Mainly, two factors will trigger this return according to Gribbon: religious education for children and stable
roots for a life stage of growing responsibility.[3]

Search for Community

Returnees were looking for an extended family atmosphere. Although pastors and longtime congregational members have generally forgotten what it's like to be a stranger in an unfamiliar group and an unknown building, fellowship and belonging are strong factors in church membership. Friendship and a network of support are magnets for the unchurched.

Personal Crisis

When life tumbles in and persons feel vulnerable, the church is a stable resource.

Feeling of Emptiness

Longing, void, something's missing, tired of the grind, brokenness inside me—that's what roughly 7 percent of the interviewees reported. What they wanted was contact and caring. Women predominated this concern by a three to one margin.

End of Rebellion

Some 8 percent of the respondents felt a need to go home again spiritually. Like rebels laying down their arms, they reconciled their battle with the church. They had experienced a closing of the in, out, back again circle.

Journey Toward Faith

Chance readings, college courses, and intense discussions with committed Christians spurred 6 percent of the respondent's returning-to-church pilgrimages.

Response to Evangelism

Formal outreach efforts resulted in the conversion of 10 of Rauff's 180.

Reaction to Guilt and Fear

The terrors of hell and the desire to wipe life's slate clean and start over caused some 3 percent to return to church.

God's *Kairos*

God's time of salvation was the reason about 7 percent of the respondents gave for turning to the church.

Church Programs and Sacred Events

A counseling ministry or Scouts, on the one hand, and weddings and funerals, on the other, provided the breakthrough needed to draw roughly 11 percent into congregational involvement.

Influence of Pastors

Home visits, hospital contacts, and the willingness to discuss tough religious questions allowed pastors to make an impact on about 7 percent of the unchurched.

Rauff's discoveries tell us at least three things about evangelizing the unchurched. (1) They are diverse folk. (2) There is no simple way to reach such a pluralistic group (in spite of the counsel of some church growth specialists). (3) But they can be reached for Christ and the church. Rauff gives us a toehold for developing a range of strategies. The "in school" helps us grapple with our unchurched audiences concretely.

In fact, launching our evangelism and ministry efforts from the foundations of Hale and Rauff, three "next steps" can be taken by us. First, we can refine a spectrum of outreach strategies tailored for differing hard-to-reach groups. Second, we can commit and train for the task of global evangelism. Third, we can get to work, for according to a friend, "all planning finally degenerates into work."

Hard-Hat Area: Demolition in Process

But before the work is tackled, some barriers must be confronted. Without trying to exhaust the list of barriers, let us illustrate some types of barriers.

Some barriers are *in our heads.* For example, each of us has blind spots. There are persons or groups or situations to which we don't respond. They simply don't register with us.

Hypocrisy is the charge most regularly leveled at church members. Jesus was tough on hypocrites (Matt. 23). Hypocrites are characterized as play actors, persons whose preaching and practicing don't mesh. One commentator suggested a different interpretation. He claimed the hypocrites in the New Testament were persons with blind spots.[4] Although mistaken, they believed their viewpoints so deeply that they were blinded to other possibilities. When we have blind spots regarding groups or persons, we aren't apt to minister to them or evangelize them. We'll have neither eyes that register them or ears that hear their cries of pain.

Other barriers are *congregational.* The unchurched, for instance, often believe the church is a self-serving institution, focused on its own survival. Many of the unchurched feel the church is more interested in "serve-us" than service. Whether the church is in fact ingrown or not is beside the point; the unchurched's feelings create barriers to evangelism. These real or imagined barriers must be faced and dealt with.

Some barriers relate to the *lack of orthodoxy,* or incorrect theology. Christians are generally aware that evangelism is a basic spiritual gift. However, some of us have narrowed the evangelistic gift to harvesting only. The truth is that full-orbed evangelism involves planting and cultivating as well as harvesting. All elements are important because the Holy Spirit actively guides the entire process, according to Paul (1 Cor. 3:6-9). No Christian is unimportant to the evangelistic enterprise.

Still other barriers grow out of a *lack of orthopraxy,* or unhealthy practices in ministry. For instance, have we counted too heavily on the evangelistic sermon and too little on the face-to-face visit? If this question receives a yes answer, better balance is needed between the public proclamation of the good news and the private sharing of it.

Whether the barriers we've erected to reaching churchless persons are attitudes or actions, they should be broken down. No Christian or church dares to be a barrier to evangelism. If unchurched persons decide not to become Christians, that risk is theirs alone. But we should be faithful in persuasively presenting the gospel at a time and in a manner appealing to the hard-to-reach person. The bottom line is this: We should share the gospel and leave the response to the hearer. Any barriers to the gospel which may develop should originate with the unchurched, not in the body of Christ.

Wanted: Bridge Builders

Jesus was a bridge person. Bridges are architechitural devices to get you across a barrier. Bridges allow you to move from where you are to where you want to be. Jesus helped a diverse group of persons bridge the barriers in their lives. Whether the barriers were intellectual (as with Nicodemus in John 3), moral (as with the woman at the well in John 4), or racial (as with the Syrohoenician woman in Mark 7 or the Greeks in John 12), Jesus bridged those barriers with His personality and His message.

Jesus was especially effective at communicating the gospel to the unchurched of His world. The common people heard Jesus gladly (Mark 12:37) and appreciated the authority of His teaching (Mark 1:22). Jesus contrasted the complexity of organized religion's requirements with the humble service and simplicity God asks for (Matt. 23:1-12). Formal religion had become too complicated and ritualized for the man on the street.

Ironically, those who represented the religious establishment of Jesus' day rejected Him. They accused Jesus of enjoying the company of sinners (Mark 2:16), of being a drunkard and a glutton (Matt. 11:18), of breaking the sabbath laws (Matt. 12:1-8), of belonging to Satan (Mark 3:22-30), and of inciting blasphemy (Matt. 21:14-15). Finally, of course, they joined in the plot and process of condemning, torturing, and executing Jesus as He had foreseen (Matt. 16:21; 20:18). For the Pharisees and the Jews, Jesus was experienced as a barrier instead of a bridge. That raises a painful question. Are we as modern church leaders so out of touch with the unchurched that we're sometimes barriers rather than bridges?

Evangelism as a Balancing Act

If we are to build bridges to the unchurched, we will need to practice balanced evangelism. Three aspects of presenting the gospel especially need balance if we are to reach the varied subgroups of hard-to-reach Americans.

Settings

The settings of evangelism should be balanced. Public preaching and private witnessing should be equalized. Proclaiming the good news in the setting of corporate worship has been and will remain a basic evangelism approach. But the fact is, not all of the unchurched are going to sit in congregations and invite the gospel to impact them: Preaching sermons alone won't reach the hard-to-reach. We'll have to go onto their turf and translate the gospel into terms understandable to them. "Come to church" should be balanced with "May I come in and visit with you?" if we're to witness effectively to America's unchurched millions.

Styles

The styles of evangelistic presentation should be balanced too. Some persons respond well to "go-and-tell" evangelism, a Great Commission style of directly telling others about Jesus (Matt. 28:19-20). Most evangelical Christians have used this approach of hard-sell witnessing throughout our history, with success at many points.

But we probably need to legitimize and train our church members to do "live-and-listen" evangelism better. Simon Peter described an evangelistic approach which stressed the pure life as a deliberate, though quiet, witness. He noted that the wholesome life-style served the purpose of stimulating the unchurched person to ask religious questions. When the questions were raised, Peter directed, "Always be prepared to make a defense to any one who calls you to account for the hope that is in you" (1 Pet. 3:15). Life-style evangelism may be our most effective strategy in reaching some unchurched subgroups. We'll have to practice what we preach patiently. Then, when questions are asked, we'll have to preach what we practice instantly.

The apostle Peter demonstrated the balance we need. At Pentecost, he preached powerfully; in his pastoral letter, he counseled a lower key approach.[5] We'll likely find some church members are more at home with "go-and-tell" evangelism, others with "live-and-listen" evangelism. From the viewpoint of the unchurched, a strategic balance of styles probably fits them best too.

Responsibility

The responsibility for evangelism should also be balanced. Ministerial evangelism and every-member witnessing are equal parts of healthy outreach. Any trend toward professionalizing evangelism allows a lot of Christians to feel they have little or no responsibility for America's unchurched. When "evangelism is the preacher's job" becomes the prevailing opinion in a church, outreach is severely hampered. The Great Commission implies all Christians are to take responsibility for spreading the gospel throughout their sphere of influence. The flavor of the Greek construction of Matthew 28:19 implies ongoing action and paraphrases, "While you're on the go anyway, make Christians everywhere." The outreach responsibility belongs to every believer.

Evangelism is a natural, normal, every day mainstream opportunity for all Christians.

Whom Do We Miss?

Out-of-balance evangelism means we'll tend to miss the hard-to-reach segments of the unchurched. Let us paint a watershed on the evangelism landscape for you. On one slope of this continental divide, we do evangelism exclusively by means of public preaching in worship settings, go-and-tell approaches, and ministerial responsibility. These active tactics are most effective when the unchurched person is passively drifting like the Left-Outs or the Locked-Outs. On the other slope of the watershed, we attempt evangelism only by private witnessing, live-and-listen approaches, and every-member responsibility. Where persons are actively set against the church, the congregation deliberately and patiently offers its life for inspection and evaluation. As a result, the Drop-Outs and the Opt-Outs are more likely to be reached.

The watershed image divides evangelistic tactics and points out the necessity for Christians becoming all things to all persons. If we don't balance out our approaches and use all of the evangelism and ministry possibilities available to us, we'll not reach all of the hard-to-reach groups. In a diverse, pluralistic culture we'd better use all our resources.

We suspect Baptists and some other evangelical groups have tilted toward the left side of the model. That may help explain why over one in four of Southern Baptists is a Drop-Out. To place this observation into a personal framework, I remember how alienated I sometimes felt within Baptist ministerial ranks as a pastor of a campus church. Because my arena of ministry included lots of Opt-Outs, I was treated as if I too were suspected of living outside the Baptist mainstream. What I suspect is that Baptists are more comfortable with one style of evangelism and the persons who fit that single approach best.

Left-Outs/Locked-Outs	Drop-Outs/Opt-Outs
Public proclamation Go-and-tell Pastor's primary initiative	Private witness Live-and-listen Congregation's primary initiative

Tailoring Outreach Strategies

We have described subgroups of unchurched persons and have earlier suggested a few strategies for reaching them. Tailoring outreach strategies to specific groups is crucial if we're to be effective.

In addition to the earlier possibilities, we'd like to offer an assortment of ministry options to be tailored to evangelizing hard-to-reach Americans.

- Support groups for persons coping with tragedy or various life transitions
- Seminars on how to use the work place as a setting for evangelism
- Workshops on conflict in congregations
- Discussion groups using the works of Christian apologists
- Regional support groups for Christian professionals like physicians, attorneys, teachers, and executives

- Alcohol and drug education workshops
- Counseling resources
- Medical and dental clinics
- Bible studies and prayer groups in work settings
- Shopping center chaplains
- Industrial chaplains
- Political action groups to implement Christian social concerns
- Ministries through sports and recreation
- Marriage and family enrichment
- Formerly married support groups
- Discussion groups on a theology of leisure
- Weeknight worship options
- Literacy classes
- Seminars on cults and world religions
- Leisure ministries to resorts and campgrounds

Some of these options would be targeted directly to the un-churched. Others would focus on expanding understandings and training Christians for outreach. Both approaches are necessary. Congregations need to consider the specific interests of their un-churched neighbors and try to meet them where they are with the gospel.

To the Work

After the theories are discussed and the strategies planned, the work of evangelism and ministry remains to be done. The un-churched aren't likely to beg us for the gospel. We'll still have to tailor a witness to the needs of hard-to-reach Americans. That witness should be natural and consistent.

A little boy returned home from his first visit to Sunday School. "Who was your teacher?" his mother asked.

"I don't know her name," the youngster replied. "But I think she was Jesus' grandmother."

"Why do you think that?" his mother asked with astonishment.

"Because," he reasoned, "He's all she talked about!"

When our targeting of hard-to-reach persons and our tailoring of strategies are finished, we all have to talk about Jesus. That's the final step in bridging the evangelistic gap between the church and the hard-to-reach.

Notes

1. Douglas Walrath, "Response: Why Some People Might Go Back to Church," *Review of Religious Research*, 21, No. 4, Supplement 1980, p. 474.

2. Edward Rauff, *Why People Join the Church*, pp. 61-158. Rauff indicates percentages for some of the reasons. I've listed them when available.

3. Robert T. Gribbon, "Will They Come Back When They're Thirty Years Old?," *Action Information*, Alban Institute, Washington, DC, vol. 7, no. 2, pp. 1-3; and Jim Castelli, "30s Generation Offers Church a Challenge," *Washington (DC) Star*, 18 Oct. 1980, p. A-8.

4. L. H. Marshall, *The Challenge of New Testament Ethics* (London: Macmillan, 1964), pp. 60-62.

5. Robert D. Dale, *Growing a Loving Church* (Nashville: Convention, 1974), pp. 45-46.